CORPORATE FAITH

How to Survive Corporate America and Still
Be a Good, Faith-Based, and Moral Person

CHRISTINA FLEMING, Ph.D.

WESTBOW
PRESS®
A DIVISION OF THOMAS NELSON
& ZONDERVAN

WestBow Press books may be ordered through booksellers or by contacting:

WestBow Press
A Division of Thomas Nelson & Zondervan
1663 Liberty Drive
Bloomington, IN 47403
www.westbowpress.com
1 (866) 928-1240

ISBN: 978-1-9736-4485-9 (sc)
ISBN: 978-1-9736-4487-3 (hc)
ISBN: 978-1-9736-4486-6 (e)

Library of Congress Control Number: 2018913351

Print information available on the last page.

WestBow Press rev. date: 11/14/2018

CONTENTS

CHAPTER 1
About Me

My name is Dr. Christina Fleming, and I've been working in the corporate world in some form or fashion for the past thirty-two years. When I look back on my experience, I still can't believe it has been that long. It feels like it went by in a flash, but on the other hand, it feels like an eternity. I definitely have the wrinkles and stomach issues to prove that the journey has been challenging. Yes, Pepto-Bismol and Prevacid are my close, personal friends.

I grew up in a small farm town in northern Illinois. When I lived there, the town had one four-way stop, three bars and liquor shops, one car dealer, and a gas station. It was the kind of town where everyone knew everyone else's business, but it was also a town where everyone looked out for one another. Growing up in the seventies and eighties was an adventure. There was no such thing as a cell phone, and the landline was just called "the phone." During the summer, there was no such thing as summer camp. Your summer consisted of your mom telling you to go play outside and be home before dinner. When it was time for dinner, your mom would go out on the porch and scream, "Dinnertime!" (sometimes she would ring a bell as well), knowing that within five minutes, you would be running back to the house with a massive feeling of hunger. Back then, there was no doubt that you would just show up. Not like today, where you worry every second that your kid will be okay out there by him- or herself.

I grew up in a very Italian, Catholic home. Midwestern values were a core part of the family. I had two 100 percent Italian and 100 percent Catholic grandmothers who made sure that my sister and I grew up in a wholesome way. Two main rules applied in our house: (1) kids speak when spoken to, and (2) always do what you say you are going to do (i.e., always keep your word). There were a lot of other rules too, but these are the ones that definitely stuck with me. Resistance was futile, and you never wanted to experience the consequences of breaking the rules. Days of taking away the iPad or computer didn't exist, and spankings were seen as the only way to go for punishment. The adults in our family spoke Italian when they didn't want the kids to know what they were talking about. What the adults didn't realize is that the kids started to understand Italian. When that happened, speaking Italian in front of us ceased and desisted. Yelling in Italian never stopped, though. Needless to say, it was an interesting childhood. (Just a heads up: I use the word *interesting* when I feel like I can't say something is bad, but I also can't justify saying something good about it as well.) Whatever the downfalls, I did grow up with good, solid Midwestern values: respect your elders, respect others, be loyal, and be the best you can be.

From day one, I wanted to be a doctor. I can't remember ever wanting to be anything else. I think the desire started with my parents telling me that I should be a doctor. Brainwashing apparently does work. In the seventies, there seemed to be a lot more respect around the profession. Unfortunately, it feels like today's society does not look upon doctors and lawyers in the same prestigious manner. Even so, my parents wanted me to be the best and smartest person possible.

I was a very, let's just say, conscientious kid. This is a nice way of saying that I was a perfectionist who determined that failure was never an option. What I didn't know back then was that the only way to achieve success is to experience failure. The pressure that my parents placed on me led to a diagnosis of an ulcer at age seven. I realize now that it was probably a combination of environmental pressure and pure genetics that triggered my perfectionism. But at the time, who knew any better, right? Something must have worked because I never had the desire to smoke or do nonprescribed drugs. Also, I can think of only two times where I've had an alcoholic drink: once when I graduated from college and once when I received my doctorate. Now, I'm not saying that drinking alcohol is bad. It was just never a good fit for me. Alcoholism was rampant in my family, and I vowed to myself that I would never let my future children experience what I experienced. I do have a bad habit of biting my nails. I would like to think that is my only vice; however, many of you who know me may be mentally adding items to Chrissy's vice list.

All in all, I think I turned out okay. I progressed through elementary and middle school in our small town, never really understanding that there was an outside world that was so big and interesting. The bubble of the small town was safe and known. Entering the big, bad world was not an option, but luckily, my parents knew better and threw me into the depths of the external unknown.

CHAPTER 2
Entrance into the World of Catholic Education

In 1982, as I approached my eighth-grade graduation, my parents kindly informed me that I would be attending St. Francis Academy, an all-girls Catholic high school, located in Joliet, Illinois. Joliet. *What? How could my parents send me to Joliet?* That was a whole twenty miles away. All my lifelong friends were in my small town and were planning to attend the local high school. I would be the laughingstock of all my friends. How dare my parents even think about sending me outside of my comfort zone! I truly hated my parents.

I remember the first day of high school very, very well. Because we were a whole whopping twenty miles from Joliet, several families from small towns in our surrounding areas got together and organized a school bus that would take us all to St. Francis Academy as well as the all-boys Catholic high school in Joliet, which was called Joliet Catholic High School. My dad would drive me (and later on, my sister and me) to the interstate diner parking lot, where the bus would pick us up. Mr. Fitz was our bus driver. Of course, he was a friend of a cousin of an acquaintance—or something like that—so we were safe.

Everyone knew one another back in those days. Mr. Fitz was a great guy and somehow jolly at six in the morning when the bus picked us up. We would then proceed to two other small stops and then make the jaunt up to Joliet. I never understood why we had to be at the bus stop at six, when school started around eight, but what did I know? I vividly recall getting up at five in the morning on those cold winter days in Illinois, when I would throw on my uniform, brush my hair, and try to curl around the heating vent in the bathroom, praying for just five more minutes of sleep and warmth.

The first day on the bus was enormously stressful. To coincide with the small-town approach, I was told that the daughter of a friend of my uncle's (yes, the scary networking continues) would be going to St. Francis as well. The girl lived in the next town over, and she would be boarding the bus at the second stop. Back then, there was no Facebook, no Skype, and no personal computers of any kind. I had no idea what this girl looked like or who she was. When we got to the second stop, three girls and a few boys boarded the bus. I was kind of a shy kid, not wanting to place focus on myself, so I just sat there, watching the kids get on the bus. Luckily, one of the girls came up to me and said, "Are you Chrissy?" She had a big smile full of metal braces (no such thing as clear braces back then) and fuzzy blonde hair. She was the daughter of my uncle's friend. She sat next to me, and so it began. Funny thing—those three girls, and the additional girls who we picked up at the third stop, became some of the best friends that I have ever had. My friends never steered me wrong, even when I went into obsessive "got to get A's" perfection mode. These girls taught me a lot about real friendship based on loyalty, trust, and faith. About that girl with braces and fuzzy blonde hair … she was in my wedding around eighteen years later, and I am the godmother to one of her kids.

Catholic high school was, well, high school. High school like the public school but with definite differences. School included all the normal high school stuff. However, there were no boys in class (except band), and we wore uniforms with a strict dress code of no funky hair, jewelry, etc. We could talk about God at any time, and we were surrounded by Franciscan nuns. We said the Pledge of Allegiance every morning, and we prayed together at least once a day. You never spoke out of turn, and when a teacher called home, it was your fault, not the teacher's fault. In my lovely perfectionist way, I never got in trouble—no detentions, no demerits, no shenanigans of any kind. Thank goodness for my friends, who, although well-behaved, made me loosen up once in a while.

I can clearly remember one instance in my senior economics class. Sister Anna Marie taught economics. I thought she was a hundred years old at the time, but I recently found out that she passed just a few years ago. God rest her soul. She was a great teacher, and I guess she wasn't a hundred years old when I was her student. Sister Anna Marie had the skill of teaching with her eyes closed and hands folded on her lap. She sat at the front of the classroom and informed us about economic concepts and market trends, all doing so with her eyes closed and her hands folded. Now, she was not like this all the time but seemed to go into this peaceful mode frequently throughout the week. That is, until someone in the classroom acted up. See, while Sister Anna Marie had her eyes closed, several of us in the class would pass notes. Do they still do this, or is everything a text message now? Note passing was highly forbidden and would result in a consequence of some sort. Notes would start to get passed as Sister Anna Marie closed her eyes and spewed out the latest economic theory. No sooner than one pass of the note would happen, and Sister Anna Marie would open her eyes and transform into what I can only equate to a Jekyll conversion to Hyde moment. She would stand up and ensure that the note-passing culprits were singled out. Next thing you know, some of the students were sent to the principal's office, a trip that you would never wish on your worst enemy. Only years later did I realize that Sister Anna Marie taught us a very valuable listen. Be respectful and focused. Diversion from focus is ineffective. Stay the course and listen, even though you don't want to— all qualities that would serve me well as I progressed in my advancement toward science, medicine, and the workforce.

CHAPTER 3
Catholic Education Is Actually a Wonderful Thing

Funny, as I reached high school graduation, I realized that an all-girls Catholic school served me well. Over the four years, I gained confidence in my abilities and strengthened my faith. By senior year, I was a little less shy, more studious, and definitely trending toward the doctoral career. The fourteen-year-old who hated her parents for sending her "away" was now glad that they did so. With such a wonderful experience in such an environment, I decided to go, yep ... wait for it, to an all-women's Catholic college.

My next adventure was to study biology and chemistry at St. Mary's College of Notre Dame. My dad went to Notre Dame. With my good grades, I could enter several different colleges, but the all-women's college environment, founded in faith and family tradition, would lead me to South Bend, Indiana. Now, although I had left my comfortable bubble for high school, I was still coming home each night to the same house that I grew up in. College was a whole different dynamic. Now, I was leaving both my friends *and* my hometown. How would I survive? I'm in a different state, knowing no one. I have to start all over again. Seriously?

Still somewhat shy and timid but definitely less so than when I was fourteen years old, I had to force myself to make friends. At the same time, I had to ensure that my four years at Saint Mary's College would lead me down the path of science and medicine. I would put faith in God that He would show me the correct path.

My time at Saint Mary's College was some of the best years of my life. Not only did I receive a phenomenal liberal arts and science education, but Saint Mary's taught me to be independent, proactive, and faithful. I made lifetime friendships there. Little did I know that the women I met on my dorm floor the first year would be part of my life forever. Throughout the four years at Saint Mary's College, our group of friends stuck together through thick and thin. Again, my friends tolerated my obsessed focus on grades and being perfect. My friends would actually make me have fun. When going out to a movie, restaurant, or just over to the Notre Dame campus, my friends would knock on the dorm door until I answered and would make me go with them. I always felt that I had to study but, thank goodness, they were persistent. Sometimes peer pressure is not a bad thing. Oftentimes, we would gather in the larger dorm rooms (aka the quads) or even just in the dorm hallway to figure out the problems of the world and eat Domino's pizza. Boy, do I wish I still had the metabolism level I had back in college today. But no such luck. While we were chatting and eating pizza, I would have some sort of science book in front of me, trying to memorize things like the Krebs cycle. When the noise level reached a certain intolerable point, I would stick my fingers in my ears and whisper to myself about the number of carbons, oxygen, and hydrogen. Through all of this, my friends never waned. They would let me continue and, when the time was right, they would make me come up for air to take a study break. I recall a specific time during my senior year when I was study for a microbiology final exam. Microbiology was not my favorite subject (it's grown on me in the last few years, no pun intended). I was on the fourth floor of LeMans Hall in a single room. The windows were open because it was May and, despite what you hear about South Bend winters, spring can also be a fun time. With eighty-degree weather and no air conditioning, it was not uncommon to have the windows open as wide as possible and a fan blowing directly in your face. Anyway, the sidewalk below my window was the main sidewalk from LeMans to the dining hall. I should mention that I would often forget to eat because I was either studying or in a three-to-four-lab course trying to figure out the melting point of the latest unknown solution. I usually tried to make it to dinner, though. So back to the sidewalk ... During my most extreme, obsessed, studious times, my friends would stand on that sidewalk and yell "Fleming, it's dinnertime" over and over until I came to the window. I would come up for air and enter back into reality. Now that is true friendship.

Thanks to my SMC friends, I not only graduated as the top science student but also learned that life is more than just a bunch of books. To this day, I would do just about anything for my SMC family members. Faith solidification; strong educational foundation; and amazing, loyal friends—what more could you ask for?

Leaving Saint Mary's College was one of the hardest things

I have ever done. I knew it was time to fly the coop and move on in my pursuit of my medical and scientific career. However, I had learned so much beyond being book smart. Each day I was exposed to a caring environment, one that focused not only on developing strong, Catholic women but also on helping people throughout the world. I started to want to pursue medicine as a way to help others. Before that, I think I was just working toward a nice, prestigious, solid career. I was getting ready to further my education at a large state university, and I had no idea what was yet to come.

CHAPTER 4
Pursuit into the Unknown Educational Abyss— the Doctorate

I may know what you're thinking right now: this girl/woman has been in multiple safe bubbles all the way through college … and you would be right. However, I didn't realize it until after the fact. You definitely don't know what you don't know.

Next started my doctoral adventure at the University of Illinois in Chicago. To say that I went into culture shock is an understatement. I decided that understanding the specifics of how to treat a patient was the way to go. I ventured off into the world of pharmacology. Pharmacokinetics and pharmacodynamics were daily vocabulary words during my six years at UIC. For the first two years, I sat among PhD and MD students, memorizing enormous amounts of information and taking exam after exam. During this time, I started to realize that, at least from my perspective, there were a lot of snags in the pursuit of medicine. First, when you treat a patient, there is a certain risk that the patient may not respond as planned. The consequences were many. The patient could sue you for misdiagnosis or for well-intended recommendations. Next is the absolute worst. The patient could die, although you did absolutely everything in your power to help or save them. Hold it right there—no one told me that I could be blamed for someone dying, especially when I would give 110 percent toward helping the patient.

Within my first two years of UIC training, I knew in my heart that I had another purpose. I could still be a doctor, just not what my parents thought of as a traditional doctor. I could be a doctor who helps develop treatments and therapies and then work with the traditional doctor to determine the appropriate course of treatment. Following my preliminary exam (a whole stress topic in itself), I knew that the PhD route was the way to go. Not only did I need to memorize large volumes of information, but I had to take that knowledge and develop methods and experiments to scientifically prove my theories. That was it. My calling was becoming refined.

To be honest, the six years at UIC are kind of blurry. I studied, took exams, developed experiments, wrote a ton of papers and grants, and somewhere in there, ate and slept. I had the golden egg in sight—become Dr. Fleming and help save the world. My time at UIC was memorable but did not hold the same place in my heart as Saint Francis or Saint Mary's. I started to lose the connection between life and my faith. The environment was more cutthroat, which is to be expected. However, it seemed that everyone was on the same mission to get that degree. During the process, we all seemed to forget that supporting one another had a lot of value and depth. The students and postdocs in our specific lab were friendly, but it wasn't the same as at Saint Francis or Saint Mary's. It was a dog-eat-dog world, and if you messed up, your fellow students and staff whispered in the hallway. Criticism, competitiveness, and callousness were daily experiences. At the time, I continued to question if I could stay in the program. For a while, I wanted to quit every week, but something kept me going. Was it drive, determination, or just simply faith that I could do it? Failure was not an option, and I would die trying to achieve my goal.

During my latter years in the program, I was invited to become the teacher assistant for the second-year pharmacy school students. I would begin my experience as an instructor and educator, and you know what? It was actually fun. I ensured that our course professor had materials needed for the lecture of the day, help grade papers, serve as a tutor for students, and even give some lectures myself. My first lecture was on the mode of action of benzodiazepines. I remember it well. I was so nervous before the lecture that I went into the bathroom and got ready to be sick. Those stomach issues were creeping up on me again. Somehow, I forced myself to keep it together and spent the next hour lecturing to over one hundred second-year students. As every word left my mouth, another drop of sweat formed on my forehead. Somehow, I made it through without fainting. As the next several years progressed, more PharmD students cycled through the program, and I started to become more confident in teaching. When I graduated from the PhD program, I had a chance to sit among some of my previous pupils. As I was recognized for achievement, I heard a loud roar from the audience. I looked, and it was the PharmD students who I had taught in my first year. They stood up and clapped the loudest. I was sincerely touched and overwhelmed with appreciation. For those of you out there who went through the UIC PharmD program from 1990 to 1996, I think of you often.

That moment in time serves as a motivation tool for me even today. Thanks for leaving me with an unbelievably awesome memory. Don't get me wrong—my time at UIC was absolutely value-added. My UIC professors were wonderful and helped to shape me into the clinical pharmacologist that I am today. I still keep in touch with my lead advisor. He was tough on me but fair. Thanks, Fran, for always pushing me to levels that I never dreamed of reaching.

While at UIC, I definitely learned the hard way some of the business tools that I would encounter later in life. I just didn't know it yet. You don't know what you don't know, right? One thing is for sure. My lovely, comfy, safe bubble had burst. You may be wondering where my faith was during this time. It was still there but pushed way, way down. Who had time for church or helping others? I prayed but mostly to ask to pass a test or get through some horrendous milestone that was standing in my way. I was in a hole, and I had to crawl out. That was my mission.

Believe me though, my faith would rise to the surface on occasion. Those Midwestern Catholic values that served as a foundation of my development were still there. In fact, when they would rise to the top, it was often observed as a weakness. Loyalty, kindness, trust—these traits were no longer part of my day-to-day living, and I kept them controlled for fear of being accused of being fragile and pathetic.

Again, I know I painted a bleak picture of my six years at UIC. In reality, I'm very thankful that I participated and successfully lived through the experience. The thankfulness wasn't realized until after graduation. When you are in the moment, you sometimes can't see the forest for the trees.

At long last, in May 1996, I did what I had set out to accomplish since age of five—I became Dr. Fleming. Now what should I do?

CHAPTER 5
What Now?

As I was approaching graduation, I was, for the first time in my life, unsure of what the next step would be. Of course, being in the university setting for so many years, I knew that I would need to continue with the well-known motto "publish or perish." For those of you who may not be familiar with the scientific/academic world, you are only has good as your last publication. If you do not maintain a healthy level of publications, then you perish in the flames of scientific exploration. It seems really dramatic now that I look back, but at that moment, it was a very real motto and the code to live by.

As I continued to investigate next steps, I knew that whatever I did, I wanted to teach and mentor. Over the last six years, I realized that I loved that. I had secured a summer teaching assignment at a local community college, and one of my professors helped me acquire a second teaching assignment at a local college. For six months, I taught biology, chemistry lab, and biochemistry. Wow, what an eye-opener. I got to see firsthand what it was like to be on the other side. I had to figure out how to keep the students engaged and ensure that they learned at least something. I didn't have a professor who

I was helping—I was the professor. Weird. I encountered all sorts of dynamics. I had some really wonderful students, but as expected, I also had the students that were, well, interesting. I even had a student asked me out on a date. Now granted, I was in my late twenties, and the student was in his early twenties ... but still. I had to kindly explain that it was inappropriate for a student and professor to have a personal relationship. He got mad and left the classroom. However, he was back the next day and we moved on.

During the latter six months of 1996, I taught and was loving it. Then it hit me. How am I going to make a living? I still wanted to help in the fight to cure cancer and other really horrible diseases, but how could I do that and make money? What I failed to mention is that after graduation, I moved back in with my parents to help save money. Now, if you are someone who has done this, you will know the anxiety and tribulations that are associated with a return to home. For those of you who have not done this, please thank God that you didn't. After living outside my childhood home for ten years, reentry was another culture shock. There were some positive aspects, though. My laundry was done, and there was always food on the table. However, for my parents, life had stopped back in 1986 at my high school graduation. I don't think parents can ever stop being parents. My mom would occasionally, in Italian, tell me to brush my teeth, wear my scarf, shut off the lights, and be home by a reasonable hour. Any bit of a social life went bye-bye as well. No boys were allowed in the house beyond a certain time. The imaginary line was called the "boy line." The boy line was the area in the house that divided the common area from the bedrooms.

No boys were allowed beyond the boy line. To this day, I feel weird when my husband crosses that line.

I knew that I couldn't live at my parents' house forever. I started sending my résumé out to anyone who would review it. In the 1990s, computers were not the same as they are now. Email was in its infancy, and AOL.com was pretty much the only online provider. As such, I sent my résumé out via snail mail. I had absolutely no idea how corporate pharma worked. All I had been taught was to publish or perish. During my doctoral studies, there was not a lot of exposure to how corporate America, especially pharma, worked.

After sending multiple résumés out, I heard back from no one. I thought, *I graduated at the top of my class, and I'm a doctor. Why isn't anyone responding to me?* I was referred to a top recruiter in pharmaceutical staffing. Even the recruiter didn't respond. Just an aside, I ended up working closely with this recruiter down the road and helped bring in a lot of business for him. Believe you me, I made sure to remind him that he received my résumé and didn't bother to respond. I kindly advised that he should no longer ignore résumés of new graduates since someday they may be working next to him, helping to bring in a lot of money for the company.

After sending out a forest full of résumés, it came down to who I knew. I reached out to my lead advisor from UIC and told him about the trouble that I was having in finding a pharma position. He was able to connect me with a previous graduate who was working at a small contract research organization or CRO. What was a CRO? The CRO had an opening for a clinical scientist/medical writer. What was a medical writer? Through the help of the previous graduate (who, by the way, become a really good friend), I secured an interview and somehow landed the job. When I saw the offer letter, I thought I was going to faint. The company was willing to pay me $50,000 annually. Yeah, I was rich! After living off stipends and the generosity of my parents, I was going to be rich. I realized later that this was an extremely low offer, but the important thing is that at the time, I was excited beyond belief. And so started my career in the pharmaceutical industry, even though I didn't know what that meant yet.

CHAPTER 6
Venturing into Corporate America

A CRO is a consulting firm that assists pharmaceutical sponsors and biotech companies in the drug development process. That's all I knew when I walked in the doors of my first pharma job. Graduate school did not prepare me for this at all. I just knew that it was a job and it paid better than my stipend at UIC.

When I arrived on my first day, I was really nervous. My job title was Clinical Scientist, which, I later realized, can be translated as grunt worker. My first few assignments included reviewing several medical documents that were written by team members. The documents were to be reviewed (or quality controlled; QC'ed) before sending the document to a client. I spent most of my days reviewing documents, commenting on any consistencies, even to the point where margin measurements were off. Unlike now, where all submissions to regulatory agencies are electronically submitted, back then, all submissions to regulatory agencies were done via paper submission. So, margins were hand measured. Although reviewing all the documents was monotonous, it was becoming an extremely important task. I was starting to learn the rules and regulations around medical writing and medical document formulation.

In a CRO, it's all about billable hours. The goal, at the time, was 90 percent billability. Interestingly, you were always frowned upon if you didn't meet your billability expectation. However, little did I realize at the time, the billing had a lot to do with the projects that were coming in. Management and business development were significant drivers of the level of each person's billability. Still somehow you were made to feel that it was your fault that you were not billable. Hence, the first ironic realization of my corporate experience. When I wasn't reviewing medical documents, management assigned me to "the basement" to ensure billability. Data management was in the basement. Data management is the arm of pharma that ensures that data are collected, consolidated, and organized in a manner that the data can be interpreted. Again, I had absolutely no idea what data management was at the time. Now, remember, everything was in paper form. There was a gigantic room in the basement that held all of the secured paper files. When I wasn't reviewing documents, I was sent to the basement to review more documents, just different kinds of documents. I spent hours reviewing case report forms (template for entering clinical trial data) and creating questions (or queries) when the data were missing or seemed off. Sometimes, I would also help to perform data audit reviews and look at the stacks and stacks of paper that were spit out of the data management system. Every piece of data mattered, and I was just the person to ensure its integrity. That's what I kept telling myself. The work was mundane but important, and somewhere, somehow, I was helping to get a much-needed treatment on the market.

Little did I know at the time that I would meet my future husband in the basement. My husband was one of the data management managers. To this day, he insists that he, at times, worked as my supervisor. I wholeheartedly disagree since I technically reported to management upstairs. After twenty years, we continue to argue this point.

At the CRO, the team consisted of many interesting personalities. There was definitely a difference between management and nonmanagement. Again, little did I know that this would be a constant theme throughout my career. We had a vice president who sat in the corner office. For discussion purposes, let's call her Rhonda. Rhonda's office had all the perks of an upper management position ... space and windows. Rhonda's office looked right over the parking lot, and she could view everyone coming in and out of the building. I recall one day in particular. My friend, who sat in the next cube over from me, arrived at work just slightly after 8:00 a.m. Within fifteen minutes of my friend's arrival, Rhonda called her and summoned her to the big, spacious office with the windows. Fifteen minutes after that, my friend came back to her cube, steaming with frustration. Rhonda had ripped my friend a new one. How dare my fiend arrive at 8:04 a.m. instead of 8:00 a.m. Didn't my friend know that we had to be billable and any tardiness was unacceptable? I couldn't believe it. We soon received a memo that explained that any tardiness would be unacceptable and, oh, by the way, you can't work only eight hours. You have an hour for lunch, and you need to denote twenty minutes per day to bathroom time. To be 100 percent billable, you had to be at the office for at least nine hours and twenty minutes. Needless to say, shortly thereafter my friend resigned from her job and went to a midsized pharmaceutical company. My friend became the sponsor, which was hilarious since my friend now had the ability to advise on which CRO the sponsor company would use. You can bet that my current company was not on the list. A great example of what goes around comes around.

During my employment at this first company, I started to get back into my faith. During graduate school, I remained in a constant state of stress. I didn't have time to do anything but eat, sleep, and go to school. Now that I was working, I no longer had to study for exams, run experiments, and give lectures. My nights were my own … or so I thought. Note to self: When you are a full-time, exempt employee, there is no such thing as a forty-hour workweek and overtime does not exist. However, there was more time available now as compared to graduate school. I started to really miss my years at Saint Francis and Saint Mary's. It had been awhile since I was bonded to others by faith, and I was starting to really feel the hole that existed.

I did make some wonderful friends at my first corporate job, but the environment was cutthroat. Under project stress, people's true personalities come out. I like to call these people the pseudo-nice-nice people. These are the people who are absolutely wonderful to your face, but upon any threat that a mistake may be pinned on them, they will throw you under the bus in a heartbeat. Stressful projects are good in that sense. They bring out people's true colors, and you know who you can and cannot count on. Despite the negativity that sometimes surfaced, I was determined to remain positive and likable. I was often accused of being too nice. In reality, I was extremely naïve, but I wanted to infect the environment with positivity.

Faith in God led to faith in others. I just had to have enough faith to make the environment change. I have a feeling that you know how it turned out. As expected, I kept trying to remain positive and add value, but the environment was too far gone. The priority for the company was to make money, and nothing was going to stop that. The company morale dropped significantly, and it was too much for one person to try to instill optimism and transparency. The company's biggest asset was the workers, and the workers were being mismanaged and devalued. All the lessons that I learned about integrity, honesty, friendship, and loyalty were challenged on a daily basis. It's amazing how much greed can dictate one's actions.

Well, the day finally came. I was invited to join another company. I remember thinking, *Wow, I didn't even apply for a position.* This was yet another example of "It's not what you know, but who you know." I remember also thinking that it pays off to be nice. Niceness and loyalty were weaknesses, but in this case, it paid off. You remember that friend of mine who was brought into the vice president's office about being late? Well, I stayed in touch with her. As fate would have it, she was in a wonderful project management job at a sponsor company, and there was a potential opening for me. Project management? What was that? I had no idea, but I wanted to run away from where I was. Anyplace had to be better than the current, destructive environment. I would take my niceness and go somewhere else. And so I did.

In my next position, I was going to the big leagues, the sponsor. The sponsor was the side of pharma that made all the decisions, that had all the perks, and that could boss around the CROs. Finally, I was going to be the boss, so I thought. I knew it was big-time when the new company offered to move me to a location near the office. See, at that point, I had been living at my parents' house for almost two years. I started to forget what it was like to live on my own again. This was the chance for me to finally be an independent, working scientist. I remember the search for an apartment. Although I had lived in an apartment during graduate school, this felt different. I would actually get to spend time in this apartment as opposed to being at school the majority of the day and sometimes resting/sleeping on a gurney in the darkness of the graduate school animal lab. Where shall I move to? The new company even paid for a person to help me find a place. I was entering the big leagues.

I finally found a place in a northwest Chicago suburb that felt right. It was an eight-hundred-square-foot, one-bedroom apartment and it was all mine. As I packed my things, getting ready for the big moving truck that was paid for by the new company (sweet!), I remember my parents being sad. I guess they got used to me helping around the house, and now I was officially flying the coop. My dad, in his true Italian lawyerlike fashion, made sure that I was fully prepared for living on my own. My going-away presents were pepper spray and a shock laser gun. Back then, you could buy both pretty easily. I was told that whenever I was to be alone, I should carry both in my purse, or in this case, my bookbag. When needed, use them and then run like the wind. Just a quick note. I have never carried a purse. Even now my purse looks like a bookbag. I guess I can never part with my bookbag friend after twenty-seven years of carrying one around. Back to the pepper spray and what I affectionately called "the zapper." I would carry both items around for many, many years. Luckily, I never needed to use the dad tools, but I always kept them handy if I felt unsafe.

My first day at the new job was exciting. I was going to finally use my doctorate and be the boss … or so I thought. I started out at the entry level of the project management team. I had absolutely no clue what was expected. All I knew was that I had one and a half years of being in corporate pharma and I at least knew some of the pharma lingo. Thankfully, I was blessed with having some great team colleagues and a boss who saw potential in me. Most of my job was administrative. I would take meeting minutes, create timelines, schedule meetings, and be available to do whatever the therapeutic area, to which I was assigned, asked me to do. Many of my colleagues would comment that, for a doctor, I was willing to do all the grunt work. Finally, a place where my niceness and ethics were welcomed.

Of course, I thought I should be the boss. Why did I go to school for so long? But I kept my mouth shut and my head down and did what I was asked to do. Little did I know that this approach is worth its weight in gold. Forget the doctorate … I was easy to work with and didn't complain, and this was more important. Who knew? They didn't teach that in graduate school. Quick aside: To this date, I tell entry-level associates to keep their heads down, do the work asked, and not to complain about doing the grunt work. Although this seems to be a strange concept to the current millennial generation, I know that it will get them far if they just take the advice. You have to learn to make copies and like it before you can move into the president position!

Over the course of the next several years, I learned an

amazing amount about the pharmaceutical industry. I had a boss who was willing to invest a ton of time into molding me into a manager, even to the level of advising me on how to dress, what to say, and so on. She also taught me how you can be a good person and still ensure that you are fulfilling corporate duties. I'm positive that the lessons she taught me helped to form my management foundation. I still often say, "Be above reproach," which was one of her common phrases. I'm not sure I can ever thank her enough for putting the time and energy into me. Jan, if you are reading this, thank you from the ultimate bottom of my heart.

Sure, there was still the backstabbing and shady behavior on occasion, but the company, at the highest level, would not allow it. I learned that foundation of patterns of behavior and that it was possible to be a loyal, faithful, honest, and a good-hearted person and still get ahead. Also, I didn't realize then, but top-down management really does work. As always, though, all good things must end. Within working two years at the company, we were told that the company was merging with another pharmaceutical company. The new company took on the other company's name, policies, and so on. I also started to realize that merging can be defined in multiple ways. It was called a merge, but we were being assimilated by the other company. By my third year in the company, we were told that we were merging again, this time with one of the top-ten pharma companies in the world. In came the assessment team to help implement effective cost management within the organization. Those of you in corporate know what this means. Pink slips were coming (for the younger generation, layoff notices used to be distributed on pink paper); pink slips were the older generations' way of saying "you are out of a job." I wasn't about to wait around for my pink slip, so I had to figure out next steps.

Luckily, the head of one of the therapeutic areas that I project-managed for at the sponsor company was leaving to run a small, therapeutically-focused biotech up the road. He was looking for a person to assist with medical writing and communications. One of my mentors had joined the organization to run project management. Awesome! I was invited to join a small organization. By small, I mean, the entire company fit in a van. I know this to be a fact, because when we would go for lunch, we all fit into the head of data management's van!

Although the biotech company was small, we were really effective. We ran studies on life-threatening diseases and were a true family. This was my first experience in a less-than-ten-person company and it was great. I worked long hours but loved it. We ran clinical studies for life-threatening, untreatable diseases and worked hard, every day, to help patients. At this job, I had the privilege of working with St. Jude Children's Research Hospital. The work that I did there had a profound effect on me. I was working as a scientist, and I was helping an organization that was built and founded on faith. For those of you who are not familiar with the history of St. Jude Children's Research Hospital, please check it out. It is a wonderful story about Danny Thomas and how his faith lead to his success and his ability to give back. After working with St. Jude on life-threatening illness research, I knew that someday I would try to do the same thing. If all this grunt work led to corporate success, I would try to use the respective monetary success to give back.

Again, all good things come to an end. The biotech company started to grow, which is great. However, with growth comes interesting people. These interesting people clearly did not have the same management values that I had. We started to see backstabbing and other related behavior come through—I'll leave it at that. So when the next opportunity came calling, I decided to make the move. No surprise, the new offer came through a former colleague at the sponsor company. Wow, this job offer thing was great. It verified that if you keep your head down, work hard, and don't complain, the next career opportunity will find you!

I should mention, though, that when I left the biotech company, I received the most amazing parting gift. Early on in the biotech days, the company threw a summer picnic. At the last summer picnic, there was a dunk tank. My boss, who was a great mentor but very hard on me (thank goodness he was), was the subject in the dunk tank. When I saw that, I knew that I had to dunk him no matter what it took. Those days of working late and making me develop yet another draft of a document were coming to fruition in this one moment. Being accommodating and nice can get you ahead, but I should warn you that your inside frustration can build up. It manifests in all sorts of ways—physical stress, mental stress, and so on. I distinctly remember walking up to the dunk tank ball area and maniacally laughing. My boss had a distinctly worried look on his face and started laughing. He knew that all those years of demands came down to this moment. The next thing I knew, I started whipping balls at the tank dunk button. It became sort of a blur. You know those baseball movies, where there are three balls, two strikes, two outs, and everything goes in slow motion before the home run is hit? That's what it was like. Ball three was the magic ball. I've never thrown a baseball as hard as that, even to this day. The beautiful sight of my boss going into the water somehow lifted all the frustration. We were both hysterically laughing. When I was leaving the company, my parting gift was a baseball in a nice case signed by all the employees in the company. It is truly one of my most cherished items. It sits on my bookshelf, and occasionally I take it out and look at it. Although the signatures and the goodbye text has somewhat faded, it will always be vibrant to me. Thanks, Jeff, for being so demanding in a good way. You definitely prepared me for what was to come next.

And so it continued. For the next several years, I started working my way up. Each time I made a move, it was based on an offer from a colleague who I had worked with in the past. I kind of worked my way up and down the Eden's Expressway (basically the pharmaceutical industry row in the Chicago suburbs). In 2006, I finally decided it was time to move to consultant mode.

After being in sponsor mode for a very long time, consultant mode was a bit of a culture shock. I had been invited to start a medical/clinical outsourcing division within a small-to-midsized consulting firm. How did I get this opportunity, you may be asking? The consulting firm had been one of my vendors when I was in sponsor mode. I knew the management team at the consulting company, and they invited me to start the outsourcing business. I had no idea what this meant. However, I knew that I would have more flexibility, I could work from home, and I would make better money. Also, I knew that if I worked fourteen-hour days, at least I could work in my sweatpants instead of a suit. More money, more flexibility, and sweatpants. What more could you ask for, right?

I still remember my first day very clearly. I walked into management's office to have an initial conversation. I asked, "What is the budget that I have to work with?" They gave me a funny look and one guy said, "Budget? You have no budget. You have to make the budget." I was also told that if we didn't show a divisional profit within six months, the division would be dismantled. Not sure the money, flexibility, and sweatpants were worth it now, but what could I do? I was there and had to try and make it work.

After nine years of being in the consultant mode, I was finally at a point where I could start my own place. In the upcoming chapters, I will discuss many examples of my corporate experiences. Upon reading those examples, it will become very clear as to why starting my own place was going to bring more happiness as well as provide the ability to give back to the community. Long story short, interesting bosses can drive a person to achieve what seems to be the impossible.

When writing this book, I tried to figure out a way to share my experiences without exposing specific individuals. I'll admit, it has been hard so far. In the next several chapters, I will try to discuss the experiences without naming the company or individuals with whom I worked. The goal of this book is not to single out people but to describe my corporate experiences and the concepts that align with or misalign with my faith, values, and morals. I had some wonderful bosses, and I had some bosses that, I swear, were the spawn of the devil. It's not important who they are, but what they represent. The following are collections of my experiences and some tips on how to remain a faithful and kind person in corporate America.

CHAPTER 7
Tip #1: Recognize That Money Matters but So Does the Ability to Sleep at Night

Money. The number one goal of all businesses it to make money. Totally understandable since our society seems to thrive on money-based decisions and objects. In the pharma industry, the primary goal is patient care and treatment. However, interestingly, you can't explore science and develop effective treatments without the financial support. So, although many of us joined the industry to help patients, ironically, you can't do it without money. As such, money is always the primary objective.

Over the years, I've come to realize that people have different tolerance levels on the lose-sleep-over-it (LOSI) spectrum. There are those who lose sleep over every little thing and those who lose sleep over nothing. From a moral compass standpoint, I think it's best, as with everything in life, to find a happy balance. A person's tolerance level on this wonderful spectrum does not stay the same throughout life. At least for me, my LOSI spectrum has moved away from worrying about little things and saving the lack of sleep for big, ginormous things. The definition of ginormous has become simpler for me as well. Ginormous is defined as something that affects family, health, friends, and faith.

Is Money Worth Layoffs?

In working within many corporate environments, I've had the opportunity to experience mergers and acquisitions (M&As) quite a few times. Although necessary for corporate survival, M&As can be, for the people working within the company, horrible experiences. The one word that comes to mind when I think of money and the ability to *not* to sleep at night is *layoffs*. I recall an instance where a company was scheduled to lose revenue based on the upcoming expiration of a patent. In the pharma world, a drug can be on patent for many years. When the patent expires, the market then opens to other companies to develop and market generic drugs. Once lower-cost, generic treatment is available, the market share of the original agent goes down and there could be a very large loss of profit. Through regulatory intelligence work and other communication means, the company knew that the generic cliff would be coming within the year. If this point was reached without thorough planning and foresight, a large percentage of the company workforce would lose their jobs. I vividly recall middle management continuing to warn senior leadership about the icy roads ahead. From an outside perspective, it seemed as if senior leadership members were sticking their heads in the sand. The generic cliff got closer and closer, yet no action seemed to be taken. Then the day arrived, profits started to drastically fall, and next thing you know, layoffs galore. A significant percentage of the company workforce was notified that they would be losing their jobs. In the real world, the planning for a generic release is completely understandable and normal. However, to have such advanced notice and still not appear to prepare for loss of jobs—that's the kind of stuff that I would lose sleep over.

Bottom line: When the finance team is telling you that the cliff is coming, believe it. Never brush off advice that involves a person's ability to make a living.

Is Money Worth Dealing with Supervisory Catastrophe?

In another company, I lost a lot of sleep over having a very interesting (okay, I'll say, horrible and horrendous) boss. In this experience, I had an initial boss that was very supportive. In fact, my boss was the one who had convinced me to make a move to the new company. She and I had worked together on several past companies (remember, it's who you know, not what you know). I was invited to build a global team and centralize a function in a very large company. Although I was being asked to lead a team in a different functional area, my initial boss gave me some advice that I will never forget. She said, "If you have this position and opportunity on your résumé, it will fill a gap for you and help you to expand your career beyond belief." To my former boss (you know who you are), I can never thank you enough. That advice was one of the best that I have ever received. It served me well, and my boss was right. I joined the new company, and that position ended up springboarding me onto another career level that I never dreamed of experiencing. Thank you, Nancy, for believing in me!

Okay, back to the bad boss situation. In the pharma

industry (as with many other industries, I'm sure), attrition can be high. It can be a revolving door. Unfortunately, corporate culture is not like it was in the ole' days. Employees were loyal to their companies, and companies were loyal to the employees. Not anymore. This wonderful behavior appears to now be on the list for upcoming extinction. I have seen this loyalty in small companies, but the loyalty has parameters and rules. The days of working your way up in one company and the company displaying its loyalty for your loyalty … well, that's pretty much gone. As bad luck would have it, my initial, competent, supportive boss left the company. I was informed by one of the executive leaders that I would be assuming global management responsibility for the entire team until a replacement was identified. In true corporate fashion, do you know how I was notified that I would be the new temporary boss? In a team meeting. I found out at the same time as the rest of the team did. When the executive said, "Chrissy will be your new temporary leader," my eyes widened and I slightly gasped. What? Me? Why? The team started to clap, and I was like, "No, no, this is not what I signed up for." However, as expected, I remained silent and took the emotional punch. The "head down, do your work, and not complain" mode was serving me well, I guess.

I had no idea how to manage the entire global team (one-hundred-plus employees). I remember going to the church on my way home that day, lighting a candle, and asking, "What was in store for me?" If this was God's plan, so be it, but I could not for the life of me understand how this new position would help me in any way, shape, or form. Little did I know, God did actually have a plan!

Over the next year, I led the global team. I was far from perfect, but I was getting a chance to obtain my global pharma sea legs. I had opportunities to travel globally, present in front of the top executives, and get exposure to financial tracking and forecasting methods. I was making momentum and then bam! Another resource was identified. I shouldn't have been surprised. I knew that my senior leadership role was temporary and that I had to go back to my other leadership role eventually. But I was getting better at leading, I was learning a lot, and the team had made a lot of value-added changes. If you are familiar with the forming, storming, norming, and performing model, we had moved from storming to a performing model level and it felt awesome!

The hiring of the new senior leader appeared to be contingent on also bringing in another divisional lead. The new senior leader would be my boss, and the divisional leader would be my counterpart. As expected, everyone was on their best behavior for the interviews. The new senior leader and the new divisional leader appeared to be positive, witty, knowledgeable, and flexible. Quick warning. Do not only trust the interview process. It's really important to check around with colleagues and resources. Things often are not what they appear to be.

The new senior leader started. Shortly thereafter, the invisible power struggle started. By invisible I mean that I didn't realize that there was a competition. The new senior leader came in and was going to save the world. Now, granted, I have nothing against saving-the-world attitudes, as long as it's a positive approach. The new leader started to change processes and procedures that were working. The team wasn't clear on why working processes had to be changed so quickly. From what it appeared, the only reason for the change was because the new senior leader's preference was different. In addition, the new divisional leader that was cohired could do no wrong. Behind closed doors, he would badmouth and criticize the new senior leader, but in her presence, he would majorly kiss up to her. As you can imagine, the environment turned from performing back to storming pretty quickly. A backstabbing culture was immediately created, and it was clear that survival was highly dependent on covering yourself. The new senior leader was struggling but was very hostile toward me, so I learned to just keep to myself. It was so severe that I broke out into full-body hives. It seemed that I was pushing that moral, ethical compass down to the very bottom of my mental space and my body physically decided to show signs of daily malicious interactions.

Then it happened. The final showdown. After about two months of working with the new senior leader, she invited me into her office. I headed down to her office with my usual notebook and pen. I walked in and bam! The human resource manager was sitting at the office table. After my surprised reaction, I sat at the table, said hello to the HR manager, and then the leader started to rip into me. It was like a corporate version of *Poltergeist*. I was accused of badmouthing her, undermining her, and just all around being a bad employee. Now, I'm not a complete angel, but I am a perfectionist. I had prided myself on always being the model student and employee. Never in my life had I been accused of such ill behavior. When I tried to ask specifics about perception, I was told that I was lying. Even though, no specifics could be given. The HR manager just sat there and supported the senior leader. Note to everyone: If you are going to provide criticism to an employee, please make sure that you have specific examples. Generalities don't cut it.

After the meeting, I was devastated. I had given it my best, and the team had really come far in development. In one fell swoop, it was crashing around us. Afterward, I tried talking to executive leadership, but the new leader was the new shiny object and she could do no wrong. Here comes the lack of sleep part. I couldn't sleep well for weeks. Not only was I infested with hives, but I couldn't understand how a person could be so vicious to another person. The unproductive, cruel conversation left me with a bad taste in my mouth regarding the company. How could I stay loyal to a company that allowed such behavior to be displayed? After several weeks of bad sleep, another door opened. It's funny how things happen like that. Sometimes bad things happen so that the door to awesomeness reveals itself. God's will allowed the next opportunity to be presented, and I was going to run toward it as fast as possible.

What happened after I left that job? Well, I'm not sure I fully understand all the logistics about karma, but it can be a lovely thing, especially when karma comes back around. Two months after I left, the shininess must have worn off. I heard through the infamous grapevine that the department started to deteriorate and all that backstabbing that I was accused of doing ... the leader realized that it wasn't me (there is speculation about who it really was, but I won't go there). The leader was promptly dethroned and that divisional leader that came with her ... well, he became the new leader. I'll leave it at that. Funny how the truth often shines amid chaos and darkness.

Bottom line: When you start losing sleep because you are trying to figure out a way to please a dysfunctional, mean-spirited boss, do not linger long. Find a new opportunity and get out of there.

Is Money Worth Lack of Personal Integrity?

As I've progressed in my career, I have confirmed that integrity and reliability are critical to success. Sponsor companies do not hire vendors, they hire people. A company can think that branding and marketing is everything. In reality, people want to work with knowledgeable, reliable, and decent people. I've learned that in business development, selling the talent, not the company, will get you much further. I find this concept ironic since many corporate companies do not see their staff as their most valuable resource. It's really very sad.

Greed drives a lot. Greed can lead people to go against their moral principles. Greed can turn the best person into the worst person. Once you are in greed mode, it's hard to go back, and I've seen it firsthand. The following experience is a summary of several different experiences. I say this because I don't think it's right to reveal the culprits. However, I cannot discuss this topic without citing some direct experience examples. So here it goes.

After many years in the sponsor mode, I embarked into the consulting world. As mentioned in the previous chapter, the transfer was a bit of a culture shock. The goal was to make money, not just for yourself but for the company. Before this, my goal was to make a decent salary and, at the same time, help patients. I'm not saying that the consulting world is evil, it's just different. It can actually be a rewarding experience. However, projects are not accepted by a vendor in the name of science. Projects are accepted because it brings in money. Sometimes you're lucky and a project comes in that brings both financial reward and scientific interest. Unfortunately, those types of projects are rare.

Early in my consulting career, I had no idea how to make the money. I started to reach out to my network that I had built up over the last fifteen to twenty years and inquired about potential opportunities. This was the moment that my head down and no complaining mode was going to pay off. I could just feel it. By the grace of God and luck as well, I started to build a successful consulting practice. I worried every day and most nights about ensuring that I brought in enough money to adequately support the family. With the help of a wonderful, awesome finance manager (you know who you are), I started to learn how my billable hours were perceived on the finance side. The finance manager started to teach me the basic principles for how the money was recognized and accounted for, and I started to get savvier on how to run a business.

The consulting business grew, and we needed to start adding headcount. Just like in the CRO days, billability was everything. However, at the same time, our leadership team had to build the business as well. There was absolutely no excuse (per the company management). We had to be megabillable and somehow grow the organization to a huge success. Now, I'm not naïve in some respects. To build a successful business, you have to work hard (I was logging in sixty to seventy hours per week) and put in the sweat equity. As the business grew, addition of business development and recruiting staff was necessary. My connections could take us only so far. So sales and recruiting were assigned to our division. I thought, *Okay, this is great. We can focus on project work and additional opportunities would come in through business development.* Unfortunately, those opportunities weren't coming. We were still winning projects based on the operational team connections, except this time the sales team was getting credit and our overhead was going up. When I addressed this concept with the company management, I was told that it wasn't my concern. I was not permitted to view financial reports, and I was told to keep my nose out of it. Each day our hours were tracked, and the operations team would be pulled in for the weekly verbal slamming about billability. At this point though, new business was solely the responsibility of business development. If we weren't billing enough, that meant that not enough projects were coming in … which meant that business development was not pulling their weight. What's up with that? We are paying for a service that was not getting a return on investment. Come to find out that company management was throwing commission to favorite employees. Again, I'm not naïve. Managers have their favorites, but when it comes to compensation, it is absolutely critical that fairness is factored in. Compensation inequality is rampant everywhere, but when you can, you should include a process that yields the fairest structure possible.

The last straw was when I was informed that one of the sales/recruiting team was receiving commission on a project/resource that was the sales/recruiting member had never contacted. Basically, commission was being falsely paid out and no one, not even the sales/recruiting resource, brought it to light. How in the world can you accept commission on a project or resource that you blatantly know is not deserved?

There's the greed versus integrity thing. Luckily, since then, I've gotten savvier (at least I think). I now surround myself with only the best sales/recruiters of the highest integrity. Thanks to my current coworkers. You made me like business development people again!

Bottom line: Surround yourself with forthright and transparent resources who prove that honesty and integrity are just as important to them as they are to you. When you do that, you will definitely sleep better at night.

Is Money Worth Putting up with a Toxic Corporate Culture?

I have often tried to define what toxic environment means. To me, there are three things that drive corporate culture: 1) your boss; 2) colleague trust; 3) leadership values. I truly believe that a large part of a person liking his or her job is who the boss is. Good boss equals support and growth. Bad boss equals negative competitiveness and lack of energy spent in growing a person, both professionally and personally. Toxicity happens when all three of these traits exist. It's the perfect storm.

I can honestly think of several situations where a perfect storm was brewing. I can think of several positions where my boss was less than optimal, many of my colleagues were so into money and commission that they were losing sight of what's important, and the company/leadership values consisted of greed and making a buck. Backstabbing and mockery were the main themes. As I mentioned already, when I entered the consultant world, I was pretty clueless about how to run a consulting practice. Fortunately, with the help of some very close friends and colleagues, the consulting business grew to a success level that I would have never predicted. Unfortunately, at the beginning, I was taken advantage of quite a bit. I wouldn't realize this, of course, until down the road. However, with the increase in practice success, I started to get savvier about how business worked.

As I continued to take positions that I thought would bring me success (both financially and professionally), I encountered more and more negative entities. By negative entities, I mean people who are out for themselves and not willing to help the team. Negative entities are the ones who smile to your face and then backstab and complain about you behind your back. Negative entities are those people who give you a pit in your stomach when you're around them. Your body and mind become drained and weak. Your subconscious is trying to tell you to run far, far away, but you can't because your mortgage payment is dependent on the fact that you come to work and do your job, even if you don't like some of your coworkers.

During my career, I've had several toxic bosses. Most of them I inherited, meaning I did not make a move to work for them. They were acquired along the way. I've had up to three bosses in a one-year period. It's usually the acquired ones that make me contemplate making the next career move. I had one boss who would come in my office and yell on a regular basis. This boss also told me that I was being difficult when I asked questions about the budget and how certain funds were being allocated. Apparently, I was on a need-to-know basis, even though I was responsible for the company budget. This boss would come in my office, face as red as a beet, and pound fists on my desk. One time the boss actually punched the wall.

What's scary is that I got used to it. Visits were only paid when something was wrong, never for any positive reinforcement or accolades. It got to the point where the boss would walk in and I would say, "What's wrong?"

After several years of deception and lies, I decided to leave. Now it was just a matter of how I would depart. I decided this was the time to go out on my own, and I started to explore options. During my exploration of next steps, I confided in a colleague who worked alongside me each day. I had made this colleague very wealthy via project commission, and this colleague appeared to be a very loyal and dear friend. Well, that was so wrong. The colleague went to company management and threw me under the bus. To obtain a promotion, the colleague not only relayed my private conversations to upper management,the colleague added many lies on top of it. The next thing I know, I had a tyrant boss in my office. I recall that day well. My boss's face was the reddest that I had ever seen it. I thought his carotid artery was going to blow and shoot right across the room. By this time, I was so used to being yelled and screamed at that nothing really phased me. That's pretty sad, right? Shortly, thereafter, my next opportunity came up, and I started my next adventure. It took me about three months in the new job to decompress. Every time my new boss walked in, I thought he was going to yell, but luckily, he didn't. As for the colleague who threw me under the bus, I am polite when I see the colleague, but there are no more feelings of loyalty and friendship. I made sure that any projects coming in were not thrown the colleague's way as before. The colleague got a promotion, and I hope that the colleague is living happily ever after with the screamer boss. Sadly, the colleague doesn't realize that someday the shininess will wear off and the colleague will be the one getting screamed at. Pretty unfortunate.

Bottom line: Bad boss + distrustful coworker + horrific leadership values and approach = toxicity. Really be careful about the coworkers that you trust and do research on any boss you don't know. A leopard doesn't change its spots. Any previous pattern of mismanagement will raise its ugly head in time.

CHAPTER 8
Tip #2: Know the Difference between a Person Who Is Being Friendly in Order to Get Ahead and a True Friend

Good friends are hard to find. They are especially hard to find in corporate America. Throughout my career, I have made both ... true, dear friends and friends who I eventually found out were just being friendly to get ahead. The real test was when I started my own business. I love the quote by Steve Jobs, "You want to know who your friends are, start your own business and ask for their support." This rings true to my everyday approach in corporate America. I'm forever thankful and admire those who supported me as I ventured off on my own. That's when you know who your true friends are.

I should have gotten a clue when I started out in corporate. I had spent so many years in the somewhat sheltered existence of academia that I figured that corporate America would be the same. The same with respect to working with people who cared about my career path. The same regarding people who went above and beyond to help me ensure that I met my goals.

The same with respect to extending true support and assistance that helped me keep going when I just wanted to quit and run for the hills. Wrong! The nice, supportive environment was gone. Now, I don't want to be completely pessimistic. There are wonderful, kind people out there in the workforce. The problem is that sometimes the not-so-nice, not-so-ethical, and not-so-caring people are in charge. And there's the rub.

In the first several years of my corporate experience, I learned the hard way. As I started to succeed in my positions and move up the ranks, I had a chance to meet more and more people. Some nice and some not so nice. However, at the time, I couldn't tell the difference. I would like to think that I can tell the difference now. I know that business is business, but there is always a way to approach a difficult situation in the most compassionate way possible. Apparently, compassion was not on the syllabus in Management 101.

I recall my very first aha moment of the not-so-nice approach. One day, my supervisor at the time asked me to create a presentation. This is back in the day when computers were becoming popular but companies seemed to still feel comfortable working with paper. I remember how excited I was that my supervisor had asked me to perform this activity because it was a presentation that would be visible to senior management. I worked hard, stayed late, and when I was finished, I knew that the presentation was exactly what my supervisor wanted. I printed the presentation, placed it in a binder, and brought the presentation to the supervisor's office. The supervisor glanced through it quickly, yelled that his mind was changed, and threw the binder at my head. Luckily, I ducked in time to not get nailed with a one-inch binder (with metal rings too). The binder hit the wall behind me, and I calmly picked it up and left the office. Needless to say, that is the day that I started looking for my next opportunity. Thankfully, through a friend, I was recruited to the next place.

In my experience, many times there is a common factor that allows you to distinguish between a true friend and fake friend (this is the term that I use when referring to someone who acts nice and friendly but uses you to get ahead to acquire more money). I didn't really become savvy in distinguishing between the two types of friends until I entered the consultant world. After many years on the sponsor side of the business, I realized that being a consultant would allow for more project diversity and flexibility. I was extremely hesitant to enter the consultant world, but I somehow knew in my gut that it was the right move. When moving to the consultant world, I was lucky enough to have some friends from the sponsor world who were ready to make the move as well. As an aside ... anyone who has enough faith in you to make a change significant enough to potentially affect their family income is a true friend.

Once I entered the consulting world, the fun began. Suddenly, I went from being granted a budget to having to make the budget. Our consultant team put our heads down and aimed for the sky. Steve Job's quote is right on. My true friends from before started to throw business our way. Within six months of starting the business, we were profitable. Part of building the business was to increase our contract and consultant pool. We were fortunate enough to have access to a team of recruiters who could help us find the right resources. As we became more profitable, more recruiters wanted to work with us, which was great. With the success in business came wonderful commissions and margins, and our small but mighty team was grateful to have the help … but then it happened. We started to become exposed to recruiters who would argue over who should get commission. We started to work with recruiters who saw their paychecks increase because of working with us. Our small team started to identify potential resources on our own but, with the required processes, we needed to send these resources to a recruiter for onboarding. Full commission was being given to recruiters who never recruited a resource. These same recruiters would pretend to be close confidantes, but in reality they just wanted me and my team to make them rich.

When I had an opportunity to move on to further build the consultant practice, you can bet I was able to tell which friends were true and which were fake. True friends wished me well and happiness in my new endeavor. Fake friends started to talk behind my back, wishing that I failed in the next adventure. Little did the fake friends know that I received word of their comments from the true friends. Some of these fake friends even made fun of me on a personal level after I left. Funny thing is that these same fake friends have contacted me in the last couple of years to try and join the successful company that I was able to start on my own. I've kindly wished them well and explained that there are no opportunities at this time. Bam!

Sadly, throughout my career, I've become somewhat cynical. After twelve years in the consultant business and twenty-eight years in the pharmaceutical space, I've become skeptical of people's motives in the business world. I'd like to think that I'm a half glass full kind of person, but occasionally my mind wanders into the half glass empty realm. When I enter the latter realm, I try to think about all the friends and connections that

I've made, even in the corporate environment. Interestingly, I started categorizing my friends (in my mind) as noncorporate and corporate. Noncorporate friends were safe. I could be myself with them. I could be funny, silly, community-based and nondoctorish around them. With my corporate friends, I could still be some of these things, but I had to know where to draw the line. I could never let myself reveal too much with corporate friends because at the end of the day, these friends could use my flaws against me. Cynical, right?

As I started to build a medical/clinical consulting business, I've partnered with a few interesting individuals. In working with these individuals, things always start off well. It's the so called honeymoon period. Over time, though, true colors come out, and I find that my core values are definitely not in alignment with my partners'. I'm sure that many of you have experienced the same thing. During one of my consulting ventures, I started to really see the misalignment in values. Without going into details, let's just say that the misalignment became grossly apparent. I started to become concerned that the financial management of the company was in question. During this period, I had become friends with one of sales team members. The team member made me feel like she was a true friend. Her openness and friendliness were extremely deceiving. As the direction company management headed became even more divergent, I decided that I was going to leave. I had no noncompete restrictions, so a colleague invited me to consult (as my own entity) with his company. Well, through a series of mishaps and miscommunications, the colleague's administrative department sent my independent consultant agreement to my sales friend instead of directly to me. Instead of the sales friend coming to me and asking what was going on, she ran right to one of my company partners and divulged all that I had been saying. The outcome was not pretty. My partner started screaming at me, yelling obscenities, and making threats (not life-threatening, but corporate threats). I was devastated. Not at the screaming and yelling, but that my friend had actually used my situation to make herself look good in my partner's eyes. When I asked her why she did it, she couldn't answer other than to say that I was putting the company in jeopardy by leaving. I walked away knowing that I had learned a very important lesson. Never again would I let my guard down with a corporate friend.

You may be asking yourself, *What does Chrissy consider to be a true friend?* Well, a true friend is someone who likes you for who you are, not what you can do for them. A true friend stands up for you even when the situation may result in negativity for them. A true friend will keep in touch with you even if you are no longer working together and ask how you are doing. I can count on my hand the number of true friendships that I have made over the years in corporate. However, the friendships that I have made are, at the core, true. As I write this, several of these friendships stand out. One in particular comes to mind. When I was working in a pharmaceutical company (before the consulting days), I worked with a person within research and development. I'll call this person Alice for the sake of anonymity. Alice was a hard worker with a lot of skill in her field. She was quiet but mighty. I got to know Alice better when we worked on a large submission for the FDA. This submission required nine months of long hours, working weekends, and a massive amount of energy. Quick aside ... you can really tell a person's true self when interacting with him or her in a highly stressful situation. The true self comes out when stressed. Well, under all this stress, Alice continued to work hard and be nothing but pleasant and supportive in her interactions with the team. She never yelled and always asked how I was doing, which I very much appreciated. There were plenty of times during the project that Alice could have thrown people under the bus, including me. But she never did. She gained my respect instantly, and I worked even harder to ensure that her job would be made as easy as possible. As our careers took different paths, Alice always stayed in touch. She would ask me how my family was, and she would listen to all my dysfunctional stories. When she listened, she would actually listen, offering advice along the way. Through conversations, I discovered that Alice and I were raised in a similar manner. Values and Catholic education were also in her background. Now, you may be thinking, *Here comes the lecture on Catholic values.* A true friend does not need to practice the same religion. In fact, I have many friends who are not Catholic. However, having a connection through religion, family background, and so on can make the connection easier. To this day (many years later), I still stay connected with Alice. We don't get a chance to connect as often as we would like. However, there have been many a day when I'm feeling in need of support, and I will magically get a message from Alice from out of the blue. Those messages have meant a lot and give me faith that true friendships can still exist in the corporate arena.

I probably could go on and on about all the different friendships that have disappointed me over my career. Many of my true friendships are outside of corporate. My community-based friendships are priceless, and I tell that to each one of them quite often. However, I'm still a believer that true friendships can grow in the corporate setting. The key is to have your eyes wide open and ensure that you aren't fooled. Sincerity and friendliness can be fake. However, someone's action and support cannot be.

CHAPTER 9

Tip #3: Develop the Skill to Stand up for Yourself but Also Know When to Dial It Back and Be Compassionate

This is a tough one for me. It's tough in two ways. First, I was always a shy person, always wanting to please. Second, once I figured out how to stand up for myself, I had a hard time turning it off. Standing up for yourself in a constructive and productive way is an art in and of itself. But once you learn how to do it, it can be a wonderful tool in ensuring personal integrity.

Growing up, I was taught to always be seen but not heard. A well-mannered young lady never shouted or interrupted or fought back. As a kid, I felt totally destroyed if someone appeared to be disappointed in me. Everyone needed to like me and approve of me. This characteristic served me well in some respects. I was quiet, got good grades, and teachers thought I was a model student. However, the quiet and good grades world did not appear to be the standard. I was trying to live a life of perfection and goodness in a not-so-perfect world.

As I mentioned in the earlier chapters, I went to a small school in the Midwest. My hometown was a small farm town where everybody knew everybody else. I grew up in a town with no cell phones, no internet, and no computers. There were phones, though, that were mounted on the wall and had a cord that you could spend hours trying to untangle. It was also a time when you could leave your house unlocked. As a kid, you could leave your house on your bike in the morning and not come home until dark … and you parents didn't worry that something had happened. If you were out and about in the town, you still needed to behave. If you acted up or caused trouble, you knew that someone would call your parents and, when you got home, you would get punished but good. Also, if you acted up at school, your parents would get a phone call and you dreaded going home because you would get it. It's not like today, where the teachers appear to be more at fault than the students. Ah, those were the days.

My dad was the town lawyer, so our family was pretty well-known in the area. I can't tell you how many times people would come up to me and tell me that my dad helped them out of some sort of bind or trouble. It was always a surprise because my dad never talked about work at home. I'm sure that he wanted to maintain attorney-client privilege, but I also got the sense that he wanted to keep work and personal life separate. I totally get that! My sister and I were not really allowed in his office, which was located on the town's main street. For many years, I had a lot of people approach me with Dad stories. It sounded like he helped a lot of people, but at the same time, it put a spotlight on me and my sister. We definitely needed to behave well because we represented him.

So, all that being said, I can tell you about the first time that I remember really standing up for myself. When I was in seventh grade, and I was small, short, and nerdy (the nerdy part surprises you, right?). There were three main cliques: the popular kids, the troublemaking kids, and the somewhere-in-the-middle kids. Guess which one I was. The popular kids had everything, or so it seemed. The popular girls always got the attention of the popular boys and had the best hair and jeans. Seventh grade is the first time that I really recall where boys and girls started to be separate and we actually noticed. The middle school included grades six through eight, and the eighth graders were the ultimate rulers. I remember thinking that I couldn't wait to be in eighth grade. Maybe then I would be popular.

In the eighth grade, there was a girl. Let's call her Patty. Patty was a large, big-boned person. She was about a foot taller than me and definitely in the heavyweight category. She had flunked at least once (that's back in the day when you actually flunked if you didn't do well in school). Patty seemed to hate me. I never knew why. But, as you know, my dad was a highlighted figure in the community. Did Patty get into trouble and my dad wasn't able to help her? Did my dad not help Patty's parents get out of jail? Whatever the reason was, I certainly couldn't figure it out. When Patty would see me in the hallway, she would bump into me, causing my papers and books to scatter everywhere. She would put her finger right in my face and tell me that she was going to beat me up. I would freeze up if I saw her coming, and if I turned to go the other way, she would chase me. I could never figure it out. However, I needed to maintain my composure and always be nice. Until one day, it happened. I stood up for myself. I can vividly remember the instance. I was walking down the hallway with a hall pass. Back then, you wouldn't be caught dead in the hallway without a hall pass. Lack of a hall pass would be automatic detention for sure. As I was walking down the hallway, here comes Patty in the opposite direction, also with a hall pass. How could the eighth-grade teacher let Patty have a hall pass? It was just me and Patty in the hallway. I decided to look down and just keep walking. Suddenly, I felt Patty grab my shirt and pull me in. I panicked. No one was around to help me. She started getting in my face and telling me that I was worthless. The anger started rising. I could feel myself getting hot. I must have compartmentalized all the anger inside of me because in one fell swoop I pushed Patty with all my might. I felt like I was going in slow motion. To this day, I remember it like it was yesterday. Patty fell back into the lockers and fell onto the floor. She didn't know what hit her. Actually, I didn't know what hit her either. Where did that power come from? Somewhere deep down, I had the strength. It all happened fast, yet I can remember every aspect of it. Once Patty recovered from the shock of me fighting back, she got up and ran down the hallway with her hand on the left side of her face. I stood in the hallway for a minute and looked around. Miraculously, no one saw the episode. I immediately went to that part of my brain that manages good Chrissy. Would I get in trouble? My parents were going to give it to me good. What will my teachers think of me? Yet, no one saw it. Did that mean it didn't happen? I slowly turned around and went back to class without using the washroom. Suddenly, I didn't need to use the washroom anymore. Those fight-or-flight neurotransmitters kicked in, and all blood and energy were diverted to other areas of my body ... apparently to my right arm.

After the incident with Patty, I started to realize that it was important to stick up for myself, but I wasn't sure how to do that without belting someone against the lockers. And so my education on how to stand up for myself had begun. About Patty? At last check, she apparently may still hold a grudge. When I was in college and would come home for the holidays or summer, my friends and I would often go to the local bar to hang out. Imagine a *Cheers*-like place where everyone knows your name. It was kind of like that. I distinctly remember walking into the bar and seeing Patty sitting on a stool at the bar. She turned to see who was walking in, and when she saw it was me, she gave me the dirtiest look ever. She didn't approach me, though. Guess my assertiveness helped to prevent anymore bullying. Go figure.

As I continued in my academic career, I still could not shake the shy, always apologetic, wholesome image. As mentioned earlier, when I was in eighth grade, my parents explained to me that I would be going to an all-girl Catholic high school in a town about twenty miles away. I would be leaving all my friends and the comfortable bubble of my small town. I remember hating my parents for making me go somewhere else. Turned out it was one of the best things that they ever did for me. In high school, I was in a new place, new town, with new people. No one really knew my background, my parents, my town. This was my chance to escape the shy, wholesome image. Or so I thought … It turns out that those characteristics are a deep part of me that I could not shake. It is who I am. Now, how would I make it in a world that could, at times, not be so nice?

Let's fast-forward to my doctorate era. Luckily, I had a mentor who knew that the shy, apologetic, and meek person was a part of me. I didn't see it then, but he provided opportunities for me to become more assertive and stronger. I'll admit, I silently cursed him more than once for making me get up and talk in front of people. I would get so nervous before giving a lecture or presentation that I would head into the bathroom and lose whatever I had for lunch that day. Still my mentor continued to make me publicly speak or present. Kudos to him for keeping on it. Little did I know that the more I got up and defended my scientific projects and experiments, the easier it would get for me to speak in public. It found it easier to publicly defend my work and myself. Those were some tough years, but thank goodness my mentor had faith in me. Although seeing me now with my corporate assertiveness, he may be rethinking his efforts. Ha!

When entering the corporate environment, I still was shy, but I was definitely better at standing up for myself. I was still very apologetic and always thought that I was the one at fault, but it wasn't as severe as before. I recall one instance when I was in a meeting with a team physician. I had a habit of apologizing even if it wasn't my fault. One day, the physician severely yelled at me and said, "Enough with the apologizing." Everyone in the meeting stopped in their tracks. I felt like I was shriveling up right there in my chair. It made the physician look like a jerk, but it also shocked me into being conscientious about how I presented myself.

As I progressed in my career, I felt my self-confidence growing. One day, I proved it. In earlier chapters, I mentioned that people's true colors come out during times of stress. However, only a kind and respectful person will apologize for the behavior that comes out during that stress. I recall working on a very challenging FDA submission. The submission was for a brand-new drug (also called a new chemical entity (NCE) in the pharma world). I was leading the effort on writing all the clinical documents that would be included in the submission. Part of my job was to hold everyone to task and ensure that their information was submitted on time. One day, while walking down the hallway, I met up with one of the pharmacokinetic team members (let's call him Peter) who still owed my team information for document submission. I asked Peter about the timelines and the deliverables. Unexpectedly, Peter ripped me a new one. How dare I ask that? Can't I see how overloaded he was? Did I realize that he was working every day and every night for the past several months? As he was yelling, I remained surprisingly calm. When Peter finished yelling, I could tell right away that he regretted it. Instead of acting like a shrinking violet, I kindly asked him if he was done yelling and then asked him when he would be submitting his deliverable to me. Afterward, I was all proud of myself. I didn't lose it, and I didn't punch him so that he fell into a set of lockers. After the submission was over, Peter came to my office, head hanging down, and profusely apologized for how he had acted. I learned two things ... staying calm goes really far and most bad corporate behavior can be forgiven with a sincere, true apology.

Standing up for yourself in a respectful, positive way is one of the best ways to combat corporate bad behavior. Also, I've noticed that as you get further along in your career and you become more visible, it's even more important to stick up for yourself and productively defend your position. As I moved into consulting, I learned this lesson over and over. I recall one instance when I had learned that a sales resource was making money (commission) for all the work that our team was doing. However, that person didn't lift a finger to help. I walked into the CEO's office and kindly declared that either I could go or the sales resource would need to go. When the CEO reassigned the sales resource to another account, I knew that I was adding value.

Above all, standing up for yourself and for your ideas and thoughts really becomes a requirement when you are a business owner. Also, it's important to have a healthy and productive relationship with any partners that you may have in the business. In my career, I've had many types of partners: partners on teams, partners in ownership, partners on projects. One partner sticks out when sticking up for yourself comes to mind (no pun intended). Let's call him Marty.

Marty was one of the most hot-headed people that I've ever met. Marty was very nice and gentle when he wanted something, but when he got mad, the Hulk came out. I had some exposure to his anger streaks, but he never directed them toward me. If you were making money for him and the company, you had nothing to fear, or so I thought. If he was the one in control, you had nothing to worry about. A time came when it was important for company control to be spread out across several individuals, one of those individuals being me. I would make decisions and implement them. All would turn out well (usually), but if it wasn't Marty's way, then I failed. I remember one instance when Marty got particularly mad. Luckily, it was not directed at me and other people were in the room. Marty actually punched the wall and made a big hole in it. No joke. The next day, some people were there patching up the hole. I wonder what Marty told the building management about how the hole got there. I'd like to be able to tell you that there were some distinctive instances that I can outline about Marty's Hulk episodes. The episodes became so frequent that the reason for the Hulkness somehow has been blurred in my mind. After a while, I started to get immune to the Hulk episodes. It was a hostile environment, and I hated going into the office for fear that he may cause more problems. I started to realize how sad and scary it was that I was getting used to this behavior. I thought about it and decided to fight back.

When Marty yelled, he was very condescending and cynical. One day, he came into my office and started screaming about the latest nonissue. His face turned bright red, and he paced back and forth. I decided to stay calm and just watch him walk back and forth like a tennis match. He put his hands on the desk and said, "Why aren't you upset about this?" I'm not sure where it came from, but I said, "I think you are getting mad enough for the both of us, don't you?" Bam! You know those times when something makes you upset and you figure out later what would have been an awesome comeback? I'm like that all the time, so I couldn't be prouder of myself that a zinger like that just came out of my mouth.

I quickly started to realize that staying calm was the most productive approach, and as a bonus, it made Marty even madder. Another time, Marty walked into my office, face bright red, and he was ready for a good fight. Again, he started yelling about whatever the favorite topic of the day was. Again, he got madder because I wasn't getting mad. When he proceeded to highlight this observation, I said, "Marty, with your blood pressure issues, you need to watch your health. Your carotid artery is bulging and may just burst." He stormed out of my office. Now I had a secret weapon to make him leave my personal space. Double bam!

I haven't interacted with Marty in a while. When I had the chance, I ventured off and started up my own place. Rumor has it that he is still pacing, and his face is still bright red. I hope he realizes that life is too short and acting that way never gets anyone anywhere worth getting.

By learning how to defend myself in a professional and productive ways, the bad corporate episodes don't seem as bad anymore. I'm not sure if I'm getting used to it (which would be sad), if I don't care (which would be sad but better), or if I've just learned an effective way to deal with bad behavior in corporate. Unfortunately, the loyalty in corporate has pretty much vanished. Back in the day, a company was very loyal to its employees, and its employees returned that loyalty by staying with the company for years and years. That's not the case any longer. It's very rare for a company to truly care about an individual. You often hear that "everyone is replaceable." This lack of loyalty has, in my opinion, caused a degenerative breakdown in our workforce society. It also leads to a lot of disappointment. From the employee perspective, you can put your heart and soul into a job and it may go unrecognized or unrewarded. Don't get me wrong. There are many supervisors and bosses out there that provide special recognition and support to employees. However, in general, corporate has lost its ability to treat people with respect and humaneness.

At one of my last positions, I had a partner say to me, "Chrissy, how dare you put yourself before the company!" My response was "It's about time, don't you think?" If you are a hard worker, effective, and produce high-quality work, there's always a place for you in the workforce somewhere. Losing your dignity, integrity, and gumption for a company or for anyone is never worth it.

CHAPTER 10

Tip #4: Remember That You Are Interacting with Human Beings and They Have Lives and Souls Just Like Everyone Else

The corporate world's most precious and important asset is its employees. I truly believe this is a forgotten concept among many employers. Corporate forgets that the work would not get done without the employees and that the employees are human beings who have feelings. Human beings that are motivated by specific values and demotivated by others. Human beings that are not robots.

In starting my career, I was really excited to become a manager. For those of you in management, I'm guessing that you may have started out the same way. As your management career progresses and you delve into the bottomless pit of management, you start to wonder, *Why did I ever want to do this?* Am I right? The opportunity to teach and mentor was always part of my inner makeup. Maybe it was all those years in academia. I enjoyed teaching and mentoring others and seeing students reach intellectual boundaries that they never thought that they could meet.

Unbeknownst to me, my leadership and management skills started during my doctoral program. During my tenure in graduate school, I was invited to become a teaching assistance for the second-year pharmacy students (we called them P2s). My primary teaching assignment was pharmacology. Although I was finding it difficult to present in front of others, I found it comforting to help students achieve their goals. I spent a lot of time doing grunt work, like grading papers, making copies (before computer were popular), and ensuring that the lectures were scheduled in an efficient manner. The head of the pharmacology course was a great teaching mentor. Not only did he allow me the freedom to organize and set up, but he taught me the values of teaching and how best to approach teaching the students. I got to know the students very well. As expected, I had very intense students as well as students who struggled with the coursework. On occasion, some students would show up crying at my lab door, asking for help. The ones who cried always got to me the most. It tugged at my heartstrings, but I knew that I had to stay strong and remain objective. I didn't know it at the time, but I was learning a lot about managing and guiding people. Also, I didn't realize how much I had made an impression on the students. When it was my turn to graduate, the doctoral students walked the stage with the pharmacy students. When I walked across the stage, the pharmacy students rose to their feet and cheered at an unexpected decibel level. I almost lost it right there. To those pharmacy students, I would like to thank you from the bottom of my heart. When I'm down and doubting myself, I think of that very moment and somehow muster the energy to keep moving forward. Thanks for the countless energy that you guys provided back then and to this day.

When I graduated, I, of course, entered the world of academia. That's really all I knew. I was fresh out of school. No one wanted a newbie. But how could that be? I was a doctor. Twenty-five years of education and I was not marketable. As mentioned earlier, through some help from my professors, I was able to land some adjunct professor jobs. I taught biology and chemistry to freshman and biochemistry to seniors. I was out on my own, and I was nervous. I had to teach all by myself. It was a crash course in solitary management. I jumped into it with everything I had. I even moved back home with my parents to save money. Although I was approaching thirty years old, I endured my mom reminding to put my coat on and turn off the lights. Note to self: if I had to do it again, I would definitely explore my options.

I remember my first week of teaching. I was really, really nervous. It was a crash course in management of people. I had to manage the curriculum (the student workload), I had to manage behavior (freshmen were the toughest), and I had to try and teach the students how to collaborate to get ready for the real world. I thought I had been doing a decent job until one day a young man approached me after class. Let's call him Bob. Bob asked for some assistance with his homework. He was not fully understanding the concept that we were studying. Of course, I said that I would be happy to help and that he needed to make an appointment during my office hours. Bob then proceeded to say, "Why wait? Let's meet over coffee or dinner." *What?* Graduate school didn't train me for this. What do I do now? Surprisingly, I remained calm and explained to Bob that such a meeting would not be appropriate. I explained that I was his professor and that a personal relationship was not going to happen. Bob stormed out of the room, angry and embarrassed. Needless to say, Bob came back to the next class but wouldn't even look in my direction, which was fine. As long as he was learning biology, that's all that mattered. At the end of the course, he received a C grade. At least he passed and, hopefully, learned a little something about science.

I taught for about a year and a half and then realized that I couldn't make it on a professor salary or live with my parents any longer. It was time to get a big-girl job. But how? I was still considered green. Luckily, my former professor had a connection with someone who worked in the pharmaceutical industry. Although it wasn't academia, I was eligible for a salary equal to teaching fifty courses as an adjunct. I interviewed and was offered a position in a CRO. What was that? I didn't know and didn't care; I could make more money than I had ever seen and move out of my parents' house. It was worth a try.

Entering corporate from academia was a huge culture shock. My first job was a clinical scientist, which I found out later was junior-level data reviewer. I would sit in my cube all day and review data listings and reports. It wasn't so bad. I was learning the pharma industry and all the things that go along with it. I had several wonderful cube neighbors who had been in the workforce for a while and from whom I learned a lot about the industry. Just an aside ... many of those cube neighbors reached corporate success themselves. Although several of them have become heads of companies and divisions, I still think of us as cube mates back in that CRO.

At the CRO, I learned a lot about how to treat coworkers in the corporate environment. One of my cube neighbors took me under her wing. Let's call her Jane. Jane was friendly, smart, and very savvy. She also had a great way of helping me feel accepted into the company and ensured that I knew the lay of the land. In a way, a new corporate environment is kind of like high school all over again. You have to figure out the cliques and begin aligning with the right crowd (whatever that is). Jane looked out for me and made sure I knew who was genuine and who was not so genuine.

Jane reported into a vice president who was less than optimal. I reported into a different vice president, which was a blessing. My manager was kind and thoughtful and also helped ensure that I was successful. Jane's manaer was the opposite. Jane's manager was extremely smart but was not very polished. Her soft skills were not apparent whatsoever. It was rumored that Jane's manager had reached her level through loyalty to the president rather than putting in her time and earning it. Whether that was true or not, I never figured it out. I was just thankful that I didn't report to Jane's manager.

One day, Jane arrived at work at 8:04 a.m. When she arrived at her cube, she was disheveled. Traffic had been extra awful that morning with an accident on the interstate. Jane was glad to finally be out of the car. As soon as Jane placed her purse and coat in her cube, she received a call from her manager asking her to come and see her right away. Wow, must have been a project emergency. Jane took a notebook and pen and immediately climbed the stairs to the corner office. Within about fifteen minutes, Jane was back. I asked her if everything was okay. Her face was bright red, and it looked like her blood pressure would have measured off the charts. Jane proceeded to tell me that her manager brought her into the office to scold her for being four minutes late to work. When Jane explained that there was an accident on the interstate, her manager began to raise her voice and demean Jane. It wasn't long after that episode that Jane left the company and went to a bigger and even better job … with a much better boss. Jane made sure to keep in touch, and when I was ready, she got me into my next job at a pharmaceutical company. It was one of the best moves that I ever made. I can't thank Jane enough for serving as a mentor and, above all, being kind to the naïve, nerdy doctor that I was back then. Sometimes I wonder if I should thank Jane's manager as well.

I have learned that if you treat people with respect, then respect will come back to you multifold. Early in my career, I was probably way too nice, but over time, I'd like to think that I've become a stronger manager, able to maintain my values for respect and kindness. I've had some colleagues tell me that it's my weakness. I like to think it's one of my strengths. The moment that you lose sight that you are working with people with feelings is the moment that you become an ineffective manager. The key is to balance kindness with assertiveness and to know when to bring out each characteristic.

My first management opportunity was, thankfully, positive. At the time, I was working at a pharmaceutical company in the oncology division. I was serving as a clinical project manager and was informed that I would have an associate project manager reporting to me. I was beyond thrilled. This was my chance to be a good boss and mentor someone. My first direct report was a smart, hard-working, and dedicated person. Let's call her Eleanor.

Eleanor and I seemed to click instantly. We were both conscientious and proactive and, as project managers, tried to ensure that all the I's were dotted and T's were crossed. Eleanor always seemed to work hard on my behalf, and in return, I tried to be a supportive and effective boss. Thank goodness she was my first direct report because my second one was not so optimal. After demonstrating that I was competent in managing one person, my manager granted me with another headcount. We started the interviews and chose the person we thought was a phenomenal candidate. Wrong. This was a hard lesson to learn, but this hire was my benchmark for all future hires. I guess it takes a doozy to really hit home.

Let's call the new employee Sam. Sam was charismatic and very personable. During the interview, he said all the right things and even commented that he looked forward to the opportunity of having me as his boss. After a series of discussions, Sam was offered the job and was scheduled to start in three weeks. I couldn't wait to add another member to our small but awesome team. The third week arrived, and Sam started. It was alright the first week, but by the second week, I realized that there may be a problem. Sam would defy any requests that I made. He seemed to feel that he knew better. Independence is a good thing; however, his actions would cause rework and the quality of the work was not very good. I'd come to find out that Sam was complaining about me to other team members. It seemed that he had a problem reporting to a woman. It just deteriorated from there. He would try to blame me for his actions and was constantly schmoozing with upper management, trying to increase his status. It was very, very, very hard, but I tried to continue to treat him with kindness and dignity.

The day came when Sam's true character was revealed. One day, several of us stepped onto the building elevator. Our department was located on the top floor of the building. Sam and I were two of several people in the elevator crowd. Not long after pushing the bottom to go to the first floor, we heard a big bang and the elevator started to free fall. You know how people tell you that, when in danger, your life flashes before you and everything goes in slow motion. Well, it's totally true. As the elevator was falling, I had flashbacks of family and friends. But I was still aware of my surroundings and quickly served as a shield of protection over two of my colleagues. I never wish anyone to be in danger, but it is in times of danger that someone's true character can be seen. Looking back, I was happy that my instinct was to protect others and not just protect myself. Fortunately, the safety brake stopped us from falling the full way down. We didn't crash at the bottom, but we did fall many stories. Firemen pried the door open and lifted us out, which was an interesting experience. As for Sam, he acted as predicted. When the elevator was falling, he fended for himself. Instead of helping others, he clearly tried to help himself. He also insisted that he be the first one lifted out of the elevator by the fireman. Once we were all out of the elevator, we were instructed to go to the occupational health office to get checked out. Being hardheaded, I went back to work until my boss told me that the occupational health visit was not an option. I reluctantly went.

Following the accident, several of us had sprains and minor injuries. From what I recall, everyone mended in the expected amount of time. But not Sam. He claimed debilitating injury. Now, don't get me wrong. The event was serious, and injuries were absolutely expected. Maybe it was Sam's threat of lawsuit that stood apart from how the other team members reacted. After that, Sam did not return to work. About a year later, he showed up at another company, performing the same role, and hopefully reporting into a male boss. As for my health, I would like to think that the whole experience made me a wiser manager. The primary lesson: Treat others like you would like to be treated, even if the others are not so generous in returning the treatment. Good does win in the end.

As I continued to grow from my management experiences, I promised myself one thing. I would always stay true to my values, even if it meant that those values were not aligned with the company or management. One time, I had a boss tell me that you get hardened to reprimanding and firing people. You get used to it. Get used to it? I have never gotten used to it. I definitely got better at it as time went on, but I never got used to the horrible feeling that you have just devastated someone's world, someone's livelihood, someone's family. Yes, the person may have not been productive or the right fit for the company/ team, but that person has a family that is depending on them. If I could find an option to reassign the resource or, heaven forbid, be truthful with the person so that he or she could exit gracefully from the organization, then I tried that. Firing is, unfortunately, a necessary thing. However, I always believed that if you could part ways amicably, then you should try. There are some bad eggs out there who take advantage of people and try to get something for nothing. I couldn't agree more. The tricky part is trying to identify those individuals before they become part of your team. At the end of the day, you can try and hire the best people possible, but it sometimes doesn't work out. If you hire based on character, personality, and experience, you have a better chance of hiring a successful employee.

I'll leave this chapter with one final story. I was managing a clinical outsourcing team and a company that had a not-so-optimal owner. The owner had an angry and mean streak like no other. One of our clinical team members had called to let us know that her husband had been admitted into the hospital with an illness, and it didn't look like he was going to make it. She asked for some flexibility on her schedule because she was sitting with him at the hospital and trying to take care of their two children at the same time. As her manager, I told her "of course" and the team would cover while she was offline. Every day, the employee would text or email, providing a status update. She would also check in to see if there were any deliverables required. She would try to work on them while she was at the hospital. Within a few days, a client called with a question. Unfortunately, the only one who could help was the employee who was unavailable. When I explained to the client that the employee had a personal situation and that we would try to address it, our company owner went nuts. The owner demanded that the employee physically come into the office to discuss the matter or she was fired. He had a letter messengered to her and ensured that one of our senior executives leave her a message as such. I absolutely refused to make the call. I guess I was lucky that I wasn't fired right there on the spot. The employee called the next day to say that she wouldn't be in. Her husband was scheduled to have emergency surgery, and she needed to be at the hospital. She offered to call in to the meeting but couldn't be there in person. With one fell swoop, the employee was fired. A cynic might say, "Well, maybe her husband really wasn't in the hospital. Maybe she was lying to get out of work." I need to tell you that the employee was a model employee, did good work, and was always responsive. Also, I know for a fact that her husband was critically ill since I tried to send flowers on behalf of the team and was told that flowers could not be sent into the intensive care unit.

I was absolutely appalled at the owner's behavior. How could someone be so inhumane and at the same time so successful? Did success correlate with insensitivity and inhumaneness? If it did, I wanted no part of it. Fortunately, several years later, I saw the employee at an event. I didn't know what to say to her since our last interaction was when she was fired. She gave me a big hug and asked how I was doing. I was shocked. What, no cussing or yelling? I asked her how her husband was doing. She said that it had been a long recovery, but he was still with us and that the last year had been a major challenge for her and her family. Then she did something that I wasn't expecting. She thanked me. She thanked me for being so understanding during her husband's hospitalization and for being a good and effective manager. She realized that the owner was the devil's spawn and that it was a blessing that she moved on from the company. She has a great job, making better money, and can be home enough to help her children through the roughness. I almost lost it right there. It made me realize that you can be effective at your job and kind at the same time. Imagine that. I think of that employee often. When work toxicity rears its ugly head, I think back to my conversation with her and know that maintaining values can overcome the toxicity.

Throughout my career, I've managed more than five hundred people. There were a lot of good, productive employees, and there were also many ineffective, nonproductive employees. All of them helped me become the manager that I am today. Without the not-so-optimal employees, I would have never learned how to toughen up. With the optimal employees, I learned that treating people like human beings and not robots can be reciprocated and come back to you a millionfold. For those of you who thought I was too nice, thank you. Thank you for recognizing that humanity and empathy, along with understanding and kindness, can help on your way to climbing the corporate ladder of success.

CHAPTER 11

Tip #5: Understand That Corporate Emergencies Are Not at the Same Level as Someone Bleeding or Dying

I love the proverb, "Bad planning on your part does not constitute an emergency on my part." I first saw this quote posted in someone's cube when I was starting out on my career path. It always stuck with me for some reason. Maybe it's because I'm a compulsive planner and fear that I will be forced in last-minute planning, which can result in mistakes.

I know that you will be surprised at this, but I was a megaplanner as a student. I know, shocking, right? At the beginning of a course, I would obtain the syllabus and plan out the entire semester. When a test was announced, I would start studying that night and would work a little every night to build on my knowledge. The goal was to know everything two days before the test and then review the night before. Nothing new should be learned the night before. I look back now and realize that I didn't have to be so intense, but hindsight is twenty-twenty.

I always envied my friends who could cram the night before a test. They always seemed so much more well-adjusted than me. They didn't seem to worry about the test and always seemed to do extremely well on the exam. They seemed to have a social and personal life. All I did was study. Years later, when speaking with these friends, I found out that they admired me for studying so hard. They still worried over the test but were driven by the rush of cramming the night before. So my perception had been incorrect this whole time. I realized to each his own. However, I don't think I could ever get used to cramming the night before. My nerves couldn't take it.

Little did I know that the corporate world would include the same type of behaviors. There are those who plan, plan, plan and prepare for the worst outcome, just in case. Then there are those who wait until the last second and try to produce a deliverable in record time (let's call them crammers). I'm guessing that these latter people were the ones who crammed the night before a test in school.

I've worked for many types of bosses. Many of them were crammers. Now, the cramming was not always their fault. In the pharmaceutical industry (as I'm sure there is in other industries), there is always a shortage of resources and help. To help maintain the bottom line, you have to do more with less. So all of us tend to be crammers, even if inherently we are not. The key is to know when you can plan and when you need to cram. There is a fine balance between them.

The annoyance comes when there was an opportunity to plan but no planning was done. Many times, the result is people running around like their hair is on fire, making unrealistic demands and requests. When this happened early in my career, I jumped right into the chaos. You know in movies when someone says "don't panic" to a crowd and then the crowd flips out? I was one of those people in the crowd. My boss would yell, and I would become a nervous wreck. Then I would make my team upset, and the trickle-down effects continued until it reached the most junior-level person. Unfortunately, that person had nowhere to transfer the chaos. I always felt bad for that person at the end of the chaos line.

I can't tell you the countless number of hours that have been spent in the general workplace on emergencies that were later determined to be trivial. However, at the time, the incident seemed like it would affect all of humankind and that life as we know it would end if the problem wasn't fixed. Over time, I learned to categorize these emergencies at different levels. The most important level was if you asked yourself, *Is someone bleeding or dying?* and the answer was yes. Then it was a true emergency. All other matters could be filed as urgent but not critical. This is the only way that I could manage the stress that was placed by the crammers or what I later also classified as overreactors.

One story comes to the forefront of my mind. When I first started out in pharmaceutical consulting, I learned a lot about client behavior. I had always been the client, and now I was the vendor. When I was the client, I tried to treat vendors and consultants with respect and dignity. Well, I guess I was rare! The real world consisted of many not-so-respectful clients. There were days that clients yelled, screamed, even demeaned me and my staff. Most of the time, these clients acted this way because they were under a lot of stress from their management. Maybe, as the vendor, I was the only one that they could transfer their tension to … who knows.

Our team had been working on a regulatory submission that was extra challenging. Not only was the data difficult to interpret, but the client team was very challenging to work with. The team was not a team. It was a bunch of people assigned to a project who tried to cast blame on everyone but themselves. Definitely not an ideal project for a vendor. The submission was over ten thousand pages long with countless data fields and data points. It had taken over three months to generate the final document, and our consulting team had worked day and night to ensure that it was delivered on time. The database was very messy, and we were required to spend a lot of time helping the client "clean up" data. The client point of contact was interesting. She was smart but unbelievably egotistical. Her team could do no wrong, and it seemed as if the vendor was always the bad guy. There were times when she actually said to me, "I don't know why I hired you; you guys stink" (actually there were more choice words, but I will keep it at a G-rating).

One day we received a call. It was an emergency, and we were told that we needed to meet with the client ASAP. Upon meeting, we were informed that we had messed up the entire submission. How could that be? Our consulting team had performed a ton of quality-control checks. We had documentation that the checks were performed. What was this client talking about? We agreed, on both sides, that we would perform an audit of our work. Our team worked with an auditor to objectively review the submission against the database. The audit was an emergency, so we had to drop everything and focus on it. There were over fifty thousand data points, so we took a sampling. When all was said and done, the auditor determined that we had a 0.0001 chance of error. What? That was amazing. Only a 0.01 percent error rate. We gathered up our information, the auditing report, and headed back to the client for a face-to-face meeting.

You could cut the intensity with a knife in that meeting. Everyone was strategically placed around the table. Our company owner was sitting to the left of me. All others were client team members, sitting around the table. Thankfully, the client point of contact was sitting at the other end of the table. I could see the steam coming from her head. I wasn't worried. I was actually elated because I knew that our audit findings showed the high-quality work that we always produced. Little did I know that the client had something else up her sleeve. Instead of calculating error rate as number of errors divided by possible number of errors, the client calculated errors by page. What was that? I had never heard of that approach. The client began attacking me personally, and I tried my best to remain calm and stick to the facts and data. She would have none of that. She yelled and screamed while her colleagues sat with their heads down. It was well known on the "pharma street" that no one dare defy her.

The discussion became very heated, but I kept calm. I remembered that calmness was the best weapon against ridiculous behavior. I asked our client to provide me with some examples of their findings. With the challenging database, I knew that there were many revisions and reconciliations that were performed on the database. What came out of her mouth was unexpected. She proceeded to tell me that we had placed a semicolon in the wrong place. That our sentence format was not the best and that the document format as a whole was incorrect.

I about fell off my chair. She proceeded to tell me that she found two formatting errors (something about a hyphen and a period) and the first page alone. Okay, now I knew what I was dealing with. I diligently started to write down her recorded findings. All of which were debatable, subjective, and definitely not a priority in the regulatory agency's mind. Were the data and conclusions incorrect? Was the primary argument and discussion off base? No ... but how dare the semicolon be out of place! The client got more and more heated. Her colleagues just sat there, heads down, showing how uncomfortable they were in their chairs. Finally, it came to a head. I tried to explain to the client that the database had been incorrect and that we spent a lot of our time helping to reconcile the database. I then said one of the best comebacks of my career. "Well, if I knew that a patient had died but wasn't in your database was just as important as a semicolon, I would have reviewed the submission in a different manner. Now that I know that, I will instruct the team on review priorities for future projects." Bam! The next move was definitely unexpected. The owner of the company, sitting to the left of me, kicked me hard in the shin. But I didn't flinch. I was relishing the moment. Thankfully, at that point, one of the client senior managers finally jumped in and said something politically correct. The senior manager thanked us for our efforts and input and said that he would be in touch about the next project.

After the meeting, I went back to the office and informed my team. I tried not to gloat, but I'll admit it was really hard. Not only had we spent countless hours on the submission, but we had spent even more countless hours on an audit that was unnecessary. The client's emergency wasn't really an emergency.

It was a failed attempt at showing how much better the client than us. What a waste. But I guess that waste is just one part of the definition of "fake emergency."

Now don't get me wrong. There are true emergencies. When I worked in the hospital and a stat call (aka, urgent or immediate) was made, that is a true emergency. A stat call meant that I had to drop everything and address the request. There are stat requests in pharma as well, but these are mostly related to agency responses and follow up. Someone's independent stat request is, most of the times, not for a life or death matter. Pharma (as I'm sure many different industries) are filled with pseudo emergencies. Pseudo emergencies are emergencies that are critical to ensure success of an individual, mostly related to an attempt for someone to cover/address a mistake and maintain career face.

I have experienced thousands of pseudo emergencies in my career. Too many to count. Unfortunately, pseudo emergencies are just part of the workplace and cannot be avoided. They can be managed, however, in a very delicate way. The trick is to act as concerned as the person who is relaying the pseudo emergency to you. The key is to not get riled up and above all to remain calm. If the pseudo emergency requires assistance from your team, it is critical that you relay the request in a calm manner, keeping perspective along the way.

Most of the pseudo emergencies that come to mind focus around an event where someone is in jeopardy of losing money. When I say money, I don't just mean a client account. I mean there is a chance of someone losing a personal commission or bonus. Of course, this motivation is not highlighted during the emergency. You tend to find out the result or motivation after the emergency has been resolved.

I recall one instance in particular. I was working for a company that was scheduled to submit a dossier to a regulatory agency before the Christmas holiday. In the pharma world, it is assumed that regulatory agencies "close" the last two weeks of the year. As such, the expectation is that you must submit all your planned annual deliverables before the week of Christmas. I sort of always liked this rule because it meant that there was a high chance that you could take a breather over the holiday. Anyway, the submission was set with some unrealistic expectations. By the time that the last patient was released from the study, there was not an adequate amount of time to collect the data, clean the data, and write a coherent defense of the data. Management's solution was to throw more people onto the project, which often isn't the solution. There are industry metrics that can be used as benchmarks. In this case, management was expecting the turnaround 50 percent faster than standard industry practice. There is a standard saying in industry. It takes nine months to have a baby. Throwing more people into the mix doesn't help.

Needless to say, babies had nothing to do with it. We were to get the submission done in time, and it needed to be A+ work. That time, for me, was a blur. We worked day and night. I slept with my smartphone next to my head and, sadly, got used to getting text messages in the middle of the night. I would get the text, get up, and start on the next phase of the document to give my colleague, who had just texted, a chance to sleep. It was our own midnight relay. I kept telling myself that such behavior and requirements build character.

By the time the project was over, I had enough character for a lifetime.

The thing is ... I'm happy to work hard in the name of medicine and science. I've worked on therapies for pediatric oncology, rare diseases, and diseases with no known treatment. This project was definitely not one of them. This was a generic drug with an already proven drug on the market. Still important, but the timing of marketability was not, from what I could tell, saving lives.

When all was said and done, we got the submission in before Christmas. Was it A+ work? No. Could it pass the red-face test (another industry slogan)? Yes. Was it approved? Yes. Come to find out that the submission date was linked to someone high up on the food chain's multimillion-dollar bonus. Were the people who slept with their smartphones by their heads rewarded? Well, it depends on how you define rewarded. It you define rewarded as building character and living through an experience that doesn't kill you but makes you stronger, then yes, we were rewarded. Did we see any financial reward? No. On a positive note, the emergency (that was an emergency based on financial gain for someone else) allowed me the opportunity to build rapport with my team members. It only takes one project where you sleep with the phone to show you team members' drive, hard work, and generosity. Overall, such teamwork and bonding are priceless.

What have I learned from pseudo emergencies? I've learned that it's an emergency only in someone else's eyes. I've learned that if it doesn't involve someone's life, health, family, or friends, it should be classified as urgent but not an emergency. I've learned that to be successful in corporate, you must act at the same level of urgency as the requestor, but within you must remain calm, cool, and collected. You must take the request seriously but place the request into perspective and ensure that you provide a good example to your team of remaining panic free. Managing up is important but managing yourself is even more important. For those of you reading this and have had the chance to work with me in some of these emergency situations, I hope I've done you proud and the experience was as pain free as possible.

CHAPTER 12

Tip #6: Understand That Work Ethic Is Important but Family and Health Come First

For a long time, I had trouble with this concept. All those years of working to be the perfect kid, perfect student, and perfect employee, school and work always came first. By the time I was thirty years old, I finally had a little bit of a wake-up call. I had watched many of my friends marry, have kids, and plan for a future. By the time I was in my early thirties, I had stood up in eleven weddings ... *eleven*. If you have ever seen the movie *27 Dresses*, that was me. Closet full of all sorts of unique and interesting bridesmaid dresses. After several years, my mom took them and donated them to a place that revamped dresses for girls who didn't want to pay full price for prom dresses., which is a wonderful cause. I wasn't sad to see the dresses go. Hopefully, the dresses made eleven different high schoolers happy. I am certain that the high schooler looked better in the turquois dress than I did!

Although it may not seem so, I was happy to be in every single one of the weddings. Each of the weddings were for amazing friends that are still near and dear to my heart. But I was always wondering when it would be my time to "get a life." I distinctly recall one time when I came home for the weekend from school to attend one of my friend's bridal showers. I remember sitting at the very festive event and listening to other ladies talk about the toaster that was just received and what color is planned for the master bathroom. Typical bridal shower discussions, right? I remember sitting there and thinking, *A toaster—so what? I have a biology final coming up next week and need to study. Who cares about a toaster when I need to be able to regurgitate how blood flows through the circulatory system.*

By the time I was in my fifth or sixth wedding, I started to wonder if there would ever be life beyond school. Life when I didn't have to study at night. Life that might actually include a family and kids and a house. I promised myself that my priorities would change when I became Dr. Fleming. Well, so much for my promise. When I entered corporate, I worked hard and long hours. Don't get me wrong. It's important to have a strong work ethic and to be able to prove yourself that you have what it takes. I just had a hard time balancing that with life. It was sort of like I had an on/off switch with no levels in between. Was it possible to work hard *and* have a life outside of work? If it was, I wasn't seeing the way to do it.

When I finally graduated, it felt weird ... good but weird. Honestly, I didn't want to look at a book for a year. No memorizing large quantities of information, no manuscript/dissertation writing, no worrying about my experiments working or passing a test. Life as I knew it stopped ... and I had to find my new normal. Needless to say, it took me awhile to acclimate to the new normal, but I eventually got used to being available to do other things besides study and work in the lab. For over a year, I had bad dreams about flunking a course, missing a test, and failing in general. I'll admit, I still have the dream that I'm in high school, showing up for a class and having forgotten to study for a test or do the assignment. Yes, I'm permanently scarred, but I'd like to think the ends outweighs the means of getting there.

I started to realize that this was now my chance to have a life, but I didn't know how to do it. Luckily, I had friends who could teach me how to be social and start living outside of academia. As I entered into the pharma world, it became clear that the only way to be successful and get ahead was to ensure that management knew that work came first. Back in the 1990s, work culture seemed to be different than it is today, especially for women. In order to compete for the high-paying jobs, the feeling was that you had to choose work over life. Luckily, corporate culture seems to have evolved in the twenty-first century, but there are still some work cultures that implement what I call the *Mad Men* era (although the TV series had a great plot, and I do love Jon Hamm as an actor). This is the era where men went to work, and women were expected to stay at home to manage the house and children. If men worked until all hours, it was accepted. They were providing for the family. I can tell you, I grew up in a household like that. I barely saw my dad. He was working constantly. Although I know he worked hard to provide for the family, I really wish he could have made it to a band concert or sports game from time to time. It's a shame that work-life balance wasn't a priority in the *Mad Men* era.

Over my years of working in corporate, I have had the opportunity to see an evolution of work-life balance culture expectations, especially for women. When I compare being the corporate environment in 1990s to the environment in 2017, we have definitely come a long way in helping individuals have a better work-life balance. In fact, in the current day and age, companies that do not offer the flexibility and have not seen the light in terms of how to motivate workers are the ones that cannot recruit the best talent and have less success.

Back in the 1990s, I found that companies had a "I must see you sitting in your chair" mentality in order to consider you to a productive employee. Every day, I drove one hour to work to sit in a small cube, review data, and then turn around to drive another hour back home. There was no such thing as working from home (at least with my first several companies), and if you weren't sitting in your chair, then it meant that you weren't working. Back then, I was single and not yet a parent. The two-hour commute was annoying, but it wasn't really having an impact on my family life. All I had to worry about was taking care of myself.

As my career progressed, I had the opportunity to work for supervisors who allowed some flexibility. Even when the companies may have been against working from home, I was lucky enough to have some bosses who believed in the work-life balance and figured that those two hours in the car could be better spent. I recall two bosses who supported the work-from-home policy even when the company was not an advocate of such a policy. I can honestly say that I felt an obligation to work even harder for those individuals. They were willing to invest in my work-life balance, and as a result, I worked even harder and longer hours for them. Ironic, right? Imagine that.

Being loyal and respectful to someone who is willing to show you commitment and respect can go a long way.

In some of the corporate cultures that I've been in, I've seen work destroy families. I've seen supervisors who have insisted that employees frequently work late in order to keep their jobs. I've seen supervisors demand that employees work (unplanned) weekends and require employees to reschedule their family lives to keep their jobs. I even know of an instance when there was a severe snowstorm and an employee asked to work from home due to hazardous conditions. The supervisor absolutely insisted that the employee come in, and the employee was in a horrific accident on the way to work. I don't wish anyone ill, but I hope that supervisor changed his tune about life after that.

I recall a time when I was working on a project for regulatory submission. Now, granted, the drug was a new chemical entity (NCE) and was going to be the first in its class of drugs to make it to market. There was a lot of pressure and a lot of micromanagement on the project. We literally worked for nine months, through weekends, until the submission was filed. At the time, I was fortunate enough to be in a life situation that allowed me the flexibility. I also knew that a project like that would earn me corporate street cred. However, not everyone was so lucky. Many of the team members' lives were affected severely by being required to work under those conditions. In fact, following that project, several colleagues divorced, and I know of a child custody agreement that was negatively impacted. I also know of several colleagues that argued so much during that project that they never spoke to each other again (as far as I know). Was it worth it? I guess that's what you need to ask yourself if you are ever required to be in a situation like that.

As I progressed in my career, I yearned for a flexible work environment. As I would say, "If I'm going to work twelve to fourteen hours per day, I'm sure that I would feel (and think) better if I worked in my sweatpants." You know what? That was totally true. When I finally had a chance to start my own consulting business, I set up a flexible work arrangement. I worked at home twice a week and would sit in the office the other three days. In taking the position/opportunity, this was a point with no negotiation. I knew from experience that I would be able to concentrate and think better offsite. My new company agreed to the flexibility but never really approved of it. I came to realize that within the first six months or so of joining the company. Luckily, I had the arrangement in writing, but it didn't decrease the harassment and snide remarks that were funneled my way. I vividly recall receiving comments like, "Well, if you didn't work from home, this wouldn't have happened," or "If you were here in the office, you would be able to address this." Last time I checked, being physically in an office doesn't prevent a problem that is occurring at another site. Last time I checked, being physically in the office doesn't prevent a research and development issue at a client facility. Interestingly, I've had bosses overseas who I never saw, and I worked effectively with them. Sitting in your chair at the office does not make you a more effective employee.

For many years, I constantly fought the battle with the suits. As I was building large medical and clinical consulting teams, I realized a very major point. Guess what? All the best talent did not necessarily want to move to my home city. Many of the most talented resources were located "somewhere else."

Hmmm. That just did not compute with the corporate powers that be.

Luckily, corporate (at least in the pharma world) has progressed somewhat. The most talented people must have all gotten together in a supersecret club and made an agreement that flexibility would be demanded. Nowadays, companies are finding ways to work with talent who are not located within driving distance of the office. I have no doubt that the technology of today has allowed this to happen. No longer is there just the phone. Now we have the ability to see people through Skype, Facetime, Webex, and so on. We can video or teleconference with anyone in the world, and it feels like we are in the same room. God bless technology.

It's interesting, though. Even with all the technology and communication gadgets out there, you still have the "I need to see you sitting in your chair" people. Unfortunately, some of the junior managers from the 1990s are now senior-level management members and have not been willing to shake the culture of the past. Although many companies have developed policies to allow for more flexibility around family management (for both women and men), there are still those from the past who continue to fight against new and improved policies.

When I started my own business, I made a pact with myself. The company that I would build would be flexible, nimble, attract the best talent, and be an awesome place to work. Work was important, but so was family, and I was committed to each employee to develop a work structure that was extremely productive but allowed from people to see their kids in a play, go to a son or daughter's sport game, spend time with family, or give back to the community. If you build a place that exudes enthusiasm and recognizes that people are a company's most valuable asset, the money and financial success will follow.

I'm sure that many of you have had many experiences yourself. If you haven't had a flexible work situation, I'm here to tell you that you are missing out. It is totally possible to contribute significantly at work and still make time to live your life, despite what some companies and supervisors tell you. No matter what anyone says, life is too short. Family, health, and your own moral code/values are much more important than if you submitted a memo on time. Trust me. I learned the hard way.

CHAPTER 13
What's Next?

As I approach the conclusion of the book, I'm hoping that you feel that I have offered some good advice and maybe even wisdom along the way. Over my lifetime (so far), I've had a chance to morph into a person with a completely different perspective. I have no doubt that some of the perspective change comes with age and experience. However, I would also like to think that my faith and values have been significant in catapulting me into the next stratosphere of "getting it."

As I look at each stage in my life, I can see how the previous stage helped me get there. Of course, during each stage, you don't realize that. At the time, you wonder why God is allowing you to go through so much pain when you are trying to be such a good person. You wonder how people can act greedy and backstab in order to get ahead in the work environment. You start to think that bad behavior actually gets rewarded, and evil is constantly winning. The bad guys finish first, and the good guys finish last.

I'm here to tell you that is so not true. If you give up who you are and the values that you have come to live by for a job or corporate opportunity, you will lose a little piece of yourself every time you give in. You will find yourself being assimilated into the bad culture. Greed and wealth can be mistaken for success. Being wealthy is not a crime. Using the wealth to only help yourself is.

Most people are not fortunate enough to see that what goes around, comes around. However, I have been fortunate enough to see this more than once. All those years of being told that I was too nice or not hard enough on someone or even that I won't climb the ladder because I care too much about people's feelings—all hogwash! Of course, not all has been rosy. I did burn bridges with colleagues along the way, but I learned from it. I learned that lack of transparency is dishonest. I learned that it's possible to give constructive feedback in a respectful but productive manner. I learned that people are not robots. If you play to their strengths and help them recognize potential weaknesses, you are doing them a service that reaches above and beyond the work realm. You are helping them with their life's purpose and mission.

Bottom line: Treat others like you would want to be treated. Mentor others to be effective employees/people but also serve as a change agent in positive life approach. If you try to be the best that you can be and at the same time help others along their life path and mission, wealth (in whatever way you define it) will be within your grasp.

My best wishes to each and every one of you. Thanks for reading my book ... God bless and Godspeed.

Printed in the United States
By Bookmasters